the
1970s
Best Political Cartoons
of the Decade

If you can look into the seeds of time,
and say which grain will grow and which will not,
speak then to me . . .

MacBeth, Act I, Scene 3

the 1970s

BEST POLITICAL CARTOONS OF THE DECADE

edited by jerry robinson

McGraw-Hill Book Company

New York • St. Louis • San Francisco • Auckland • Bogotá • Guatemala
Hamburg • Johannesburg • Lisbon • London • Madrid • Mexico
Montreal • New Delhi • Panama • Paris • San Juan • Saõ Paulo
Singapore • Sydney • Tokyo • Toronto

Acknowledgments

My first acknowledgments are to my fellow members of the Association of American Editorial Cartoonists for their enthusiastic support of this project, and particularly to past President Bob Taylor, and current President Sandy Campbell and Treasurer Jim Lange for their friendship, advice, and encouragement. I am appreciative, too, of the enthusiasm, as well as the invaluable contributions of my cartoonist friends and colleagues throughout the world. Personal contact with them, many known previously only by reputation, has made this endeavor a most rewarding experience.

I am especially indebted to Robert LaPalme, Director of the Pavilion of Humor, Man and His World, in Montreal, Canada, for all his help and expertise and for making available the resources of that unique institution, including his fine staff, André Carpentier, Jocelyne Gagné, and Sergé Jongue.

I am grateful for the generous cooperation of Alfred Balk, Editor and Publisher of the excellent magazine, *World Press Review,* and the kind assistance and expertise of Eleanor Davidson Worley, Syndication Editor; for the special help of Sylvia Roth and Doris Cohen and the extensive resources of Rothco Cartoons; and to Lee Lorenz, Cartoon Editor, and Jill Frisch, Permissions Editor, *The New Yorker* magazine, for their invaluable assistance.

I am most appreciative, too, for the expert advice generously given by Steve Heller, Art Director of *The New York Times Book Review,* and Jean-Claude Suares. I particularly thank several friends and colleagues: Selby Kelly, for making available examples of her late husband Walt Kelly's classic *POGO;* and for the invaluable help given by Jürg Spahr in Basel, Switzerland, Manny Curtis in London, and Burne Hogarth and Robert D'Amico in New York. My appreciation also for the gracious assistance of John Locke, Cullen Rapp, and Ted Riley.

My particular thanks to John McMeel, President of Universal Press Syndicate, who was always unstinting in his help and advice, and for the courtesy of all the newspapers, periodicals, and syndicates represented in this collection.

Finally, I wish to thank my associate, Steve Shedd, for his unique contributions of talent and time devoted to all phases of this project, including its conception, research, production, and design; to Frances Collin, my literary agent, for her constant support and direction; and Tim Yohn, my editor at McGraw Hill, who demonstrated how a creative—and patient—editor can make book-making a rewarding experience for the writer and artist.

Doonesbury © G. B. Trudeau, distributed by Universal Press Syndicate; Bill Mauldin courtesy Will-Jo Associates, © Bill Mauldin, Chicago Sun-Times; *POGO* © Walt Kelly, courtesy Selby Kelly; *Punch* cartoons courtesy Rothco Cartoons; selection of cartoons from the U.S.S.R. and other foreign countries courtesy *World Press Review;* cartoons by Charles Addams, Douglas Florian, Dana Fradan, Charles E. Martin, and Micha Richter courtesy *The New Yorker* magazine; all other cartoons courtesy the respective copyright owners, artists, newspapers, and syndicates.

Copyright © 1981 by Jerry Robinson

1234567890 HDHD 8987654321

Library of Congress Cataloging in Publication Data

Main entry under title:

The 1970s best political cartoons of the decade.

1. World politics—1965–1975—Caricatures and cartoons. 2. World politics—1975–1985 —Caricatures and cartoons. I. Robinson, Jerry. D849.5.N56 909.82'7'0207 80–17176 ISBN 0–07–053281–8 (pbk.)

Contents

Introduction

Humor in times of insanity is what keeps us sane. It is also what keeps us free. There is nothing that tyrants and rascals fear more than satire and ridicule, and the graphic form has always proved to be uniquely painful. Freedom of expression for the political cartoonist is a litmus test for democracy. Totalitarian regimes rarely tolerate cartoon satire of their leaders—at least not until they are deposed or deceased.

Honoré Daumier drew a series of devastating cartoons on the monarchy, including one of King Louis-Philippe as Gargantua, gorging himself on the earnings of the working class. His editor, Charles Philipon, caricatured the king evolving into a pear. Daumier and Philipon wound up in jail, proving cartooning can be a dangerous profession, for both cartoonists and their victims.

A 19th century artist once noted that a good caricature is only fully appreciated by those who have been its victims. Occasionally politicians are its beneficiaries. "Two things elected me," acknowledged President Grant, "The sword of Sheridan and the pencil of Thomas Nast." President McKinley and Cleveland were others who credited cartoonists for their elections.

While humor has been an integral part of the fabric of American life, from time to time even our democratic institutions have been inhospitable to satire, particularly in times of crisis. A crisis for politicians is when they feel violated by a political cartoonist. They have often retaliated with attempts to silence their tormentors. "Stop them damn pictures," cried the infamous Boss Tweed in anguish over the unrelenting and savage attacks by the ubiquitous Thomas Nast, "I don't care a straw for your newspaper articles. My constituents can't read. But they can't help seeing them damn pictures!" In desperation, Tweed, who led Tammany Hall and the band of rogues who controlled New York City from 1866 to 1871, tried to bribe the incorruptible cartoonist with a half a million dollars to study art in Europe. Score one for the cartoonist. That time, the politician went to jail.

In 1903, Samuel Pennypacker, the governor of Pennsylvania, so objected to a series of anthropomorphic caricatures of himself, including one as a parrot, that he tried to outlaw the depicting of men in the guise of animals. The righteous governor would have preferred even stronger measures. "In England a century ago," he lamented," the offender would have been drawn and quartered and his head stuck upon a pole." There were other attempts at censorship at the turn of the century in New York, Indiana, and Alabama. In California the legislature outlawed any caricature that reflected on a person's character. These measures themselves became the subject of ridicule by cartoonists and all such bills eventually died in the legislature or were repealed.

In the following years a variety of actions continued to be brought against political cartoonists—testimony to the power of the cartoons, perhaps, but little solace to the artists. They constituted serious threats to the exercise of free graphic expression. It was as if First Amendment rights accorded journalists excluded cartoonists. The magazine *The Masses* was brought to trial in 1918 for the antiwar cartoons of Art Young. Dan Fitzpatrick, the great political cartoonist of the *St. Louis Post Dispatch*, was sentenced to jail in the 1940s by a judge blistered in one of his series, "Rat Alley." The Missouri Supreme Court threw out the case.

In more recent years numerous libel actions have been brought against cartoonists by offended politicians. Mayor Sam Yorty was unsuccessful in his suit against Paul Conrad of *The Los Angeles Times.* Even a student, editor of the University of Hartford campus paper, was fined for an anti-Nixon cartoon. In 1978 a Canadian provincial minister successfully sued cartoonist Bob Bierman and the *Toronto Times* for libelous cartoons—the first time a politician won such a suit in the British Commonwealth. Effective editorial cartooning in Canada remained in jeopardy until the verdict was reversed on appeal.

Corporations, too, have developed a sensitivity to cartoon criticism. In 1979 Reddy Communications, Inc., brought suit to prevent the unauthorized use of their trademark, Reddy Kilowatt, in editorial cartoons. It would have meant virtual immunity from effective graphic criticism for hundreds of companies and products the public identifies with trademark symbols. Fortunately, the suit failed. It is worthwhile to recall Judge Murray Gurfein's words in the Pentagon Papers decision, which might well be applied to political cartoonists, "A cantankerous press, an obstinate press, an ubiquitous press must be suffered by those in authority in order to preserve the right of people to know."

Editorial cartoons at their best, exemplified by the accompanying illustrations, are an oasis of emotion in a newsprint desert of dispassionate verbiage and objective reporting. They are unabashed personal opinions, a free indulgence of exaggerations and prejudice, an irreverent questioning of motives, and often fiercely partisan. Cartoonists are functioning subversives, waging war on the powerful, the exploiters, and the privileged. In the tradition of Tom Paine, cartoons of political satire are the revolutionary essays of our time. As Arthur Schlesinger, Jr., has put it, "Satire is morality disguised as mockery."

Times of crises are like shots of adrenalin to the political cartoonist, whose pen fairly quivers in anticipation of presidential elections and other national aberrations and scandals. The 1970s were a decade of discord and dissent, a period of alienation and cynicism. Nothing in American society escaped critical examination—and little was found without blemish—the Presidency, Congress, the Courts, industry, labor, the press, the educational system. These were years of scams and scandals, ripoffs and payoffs, and an evergrowing cast of victims and villains. Watergate proved for all that politicians are every bit as grotesque and corrupt as they have been caricatured. Like Walt Whitman, cartoonists were struck by the never ending audacity of elected officials.

Political cartoonists are the Baedekers of the political life of our times and chart the changing dynamics of society. The seventies awakened America to new truths and forced us to a new self-image. The decade began with the humiliation in Vietnam and ended with the embarrassment in Iran. Our once Big Stick shrunk so that it no longer reached the Panama Canal, let alone Southeast Asia or the Near East. For the first time, America felt impotent. Despite a staggering investment of lives and treasure, we could not enforce our will militarily on the one, nor was our enormous economic, diplomatic, and moral pressure effective with the other.

America not only faced an unpleasant reality about its limits of power, but also about its resources. We became dependent on the imperious OPEC oil cartel. For the first time, the future became a potential enemy. Economists predicted that the American standard of living would have to decline, that there were "limits to growth" and we were headed for a last twenty-year fling before the apocalypse. Americans were beset by seemingly insolvable problems—of energy, pollution, inflation, unemployment—and grudgingly began to adopt a new life style of conservation, retrenchment and austerity.

The moral morass of the 60s, Vietnam and the Nixon presidency, carried over into the 70s all but blotting out genuine accomplishments in the sciences and technology. The cynicism of Americans about their leaders and institutions and the feeling of helplessness on larger issues turned into an obsessive self-regard, which made social critic Tom Wolfe characterize the period as the Me Decade. The need for a greater exploration of the inner space of the American psyche led to the growth of numerous movements such as est and Transcendental Meditation. The sixties were just a prelude to the drug culture of the seventies. Forty million Americans smoked marijuana, twenty million tried cocaine, and filled forty-four million prescriptions a year of valium, not to mention seconal, tuinal, dexedrine, and quaaludes. The 1960s refrain, "Turn on, tune in, drop out," in the seventies, became "Give me Librium or give me Meth."

A panoply of new faces, new and often strange-sounding names, places and things impressed themselves upon the nation's consciousness in the seventies. The poltical cartoonists sorted them out along with their readers. Tanya, "Squeaky," and Son of Sam; Deng Xiaoping, Muzorewa, Wojtyla, Shcharansky, and Solzhenitsyn; ERA, S.L.A., SST, MX, and CB; Aldo, Ali, Ian, and Idi; the Khmer Rouge and the Red Brigades; Evel Knievel and Charlie's Angels; the Yom Kippur War and the Saturday Night Massacre; Manson, Moore, Bremer, Gacy, and Gilmore; Archie Bunker, Mary Hartmann, and Kunta Kinte; Attica, Soweto, Maalot and Guyana; Shah Pahlavi, Sheik Yamani, and King Tut; discos, hot pants, designer jeans, pet rocks, and WIN buttons; Mehta, Pavarotti, and Baryshnikov; Belushi, Bakke, Biko, and Borg; test-tube babies and Legionnaire's Disease; Fanne Fox and Farrah Fawcett; Rosemary Woods and Renée Richards; jogging, streaking, skate-boarding, and hang-gliding. Americans also heard about the Pentagon Papers and "explitives deleted." While the seventies were not an outstanding decade for quotes, several have a lingering nostalgia: "Peace is at hand" (Kissinger); "I am not a crook" (Nixon); "I am the greatest" (Muhammed Ali); "Dingbat" (Archie Bunker); "I can't believe I ate the whole thing" (Alka Seltzer commercial), and "Have a nice day" (all America ad nauseum).

The decade of crisis became the catalyst for a renaissance in the art of the political cartoon. There was a greater use of humor in all its forms. Humor is a serious matter to the political cartoonist. It is meant to inspire thought, and the 1970s were too serious to be treated humorlessly. There was also a greater use of dialogue which restored to the political cartoon the structural device first used by Hogarth, Rowlandson and Gilray, involving the reader in an illusion of immediacy. Gone were the rococo graphics of earlier decades. The lithographic techniques, grease pencil or crayon on grained paper were largely superseded by chemically treated paper that produced mechanical halftones. The 1970s also saw a trend toward pure brush and/or pen and ink drawings without mechanical tones ranging from the cross-hatch, linear penwork in the manner of David Levine, Ed Sorel and Louis Mittberg (Tim) to the bold black and white brush drawings as often seen in the work of such artists as Ewett Karlsson (EWK), Jeff MacNelly, Pat Oliphant and Paul Szep.

Though comparisons of contemporary artists with past masters such as Nast, David Low or Rolin Kirby are invidious, I believe there are more talented political cartoonists drawing now, at one time, than ever before. The great cartoonists of the 1950s and 1960s such as Herblock, Duncan MacPherson, Bill Mauldin, Paul Conrad, and Jules Feiffer were joined by a new generation of artists with new voices and concepts, with innovative techniques and imaginative symbolism, some even conceptual and surrealistic, that placed them in the company of their most vibrant precursors.

While this collection reflects the dominance of the traditional daily political cartoon usually seen on newspaper editorial pages, other forms of graphic political comment are included that appear in a variety of books, magazines, and newspapers, both in the U. S. and abroad. One such form is the comic strip, where politics has been taboo, with few exceptions, since the creation of the genre in 1895.

Al Capp brought social and political satire in the tradition of Jonathan Swift and Mark Twain to the comics with *Li'l Abner* in 1934. Capp's targets included public figures such as Joan Baez (who became Joanie Phoanie) and Henry Cabot Lodge (as Henry Cabbage Cod), as well as establishment types such as Senators (Jack S. Fogbound), Generals (Bullmoose—"What's good for General Bullmoose is good for the U. S. A."), and tycoons (J. Roaringham Fatback).

In 1949 a delightful cast of raffish wildlife came to the comics with Walt Kelly's *Pogo*. Kelly began a series of election year political allegories in 1952 when Pogo ran for President along with Dwight Eisenhower and Adlai Stevenson. Richard Nixon, Nelson Rockefeller, and George Romney were portrayed as wind-up dolls in the 1964 campaign. Among others appearing in Kelly's menagerie were Senator Joseph McCarthy as Simple J. Malarkey, a snarling, jowly dog, and Lyndon Johnson, as a nearsighted, bulbous-nosed Texas longhorn. Walt Kelly died in 1973 and excerpts are included from among *Pogo's* last episodes with anthropomorphic versions of Spiro Agnew, J. Edgar Hoover, and John Mitchell.

Jules Feiffer further enlarged the scope of the comics with his own form of political satire with psychological insight, and in 1960 became the first radical cartoonist to be syndicated nationally. Feiffer attacked the Vietnam War and succeeded in breaking the strictures of many newspapers that published him in opposition to their own editorial positions.

Any remaining political taboos were certainly shattered when Gary Trudeau's *Doonesbury* won the Pulitzer Prize for political cartooning in 1975, the only time the award was given to a comic strip. Expanding his satire from its original college campus counter-culture origins in 1970 to a national political stage, *Doonesbury* appears on newspaper editorial and Op-Ed pages as well as the comics sections.

"Political cartoonists in particular suffer a lot," noted Art Buchwald, "they're only as good as the next day's cartoon, which they haven't thought of yet." But every day newspaper cartoonists meet the challenge. They bring into fusion their abilities as journalists, political analysts, artists and caricaturists to make significant graphic statements on public issues with wit and humor, turning an abstraction into a concrete image. They do this in the time and space of hours and inches—an exercise unique in the art of communication.

Jerry Robinson
New York City

1970

VIETNAM: Despite President Richard Nixon's promised "Vietnamization" that would end the U.S. combat role, 368,000 American troops remained. The war widened with an "excursion" of 50,000 troops, half of them Americans, into Cambodia and American air strikes in Laos.

PROTESTS: The Cambodian adventure ignited an explosion of student demonstrations on America's college campuses. Six hundred people were arrested at Ohio State and twenty wounded. Two were killed at Jackson State College in Mississippi, and in a tragedy that outraged America, four students were killed and ten wounded when Ohio National Guardsmen fired on antiwar protesters at Kent State University. The killings fueled the antiwar movement, and 250,000 protesters converged on Washington. President Nixon called the students "bums," and Vice President Spiro C. Agnew, escalating the rhetoric, described his political opponents as "troglodytic leftists," "radiclibs," and "nattering nabobs of negativism."

COURTS: Nixon's second nomination to fill the Supreme Court seat of Abe Fortas, Judge Harold Carswell, was rejected by the Senate. Judge Harry Blackmun was then nominated and confirmed. Courts ordered their "desegregation now" ruling enforced and many school closed and others were boycotted in opposition to busing.

ECONOMY: The stock market slumped as inflation grew. The Penn Central Railroad went bankrupt. LABOR: Five years of strikes and boycotts in the Grape War ended as Cesar Chavez of the United Farm Workers came to terms

PAUL SZEP/*Boston Globe*

with the California growers. *SPACE:* A mishap aborted the Apollo 13 lunar landing, but heroic maneuvers in space returned the astronauts safely. *CELE-BRATIONS:* April 22, millions of Americans partcipated in antipollution activities to mark the first Earth Day. October 22, the United Nations observed its twenty-fifth birthday.

CHILE: Salvador Allende Gossens became the first Marxist in Latin America to win the presidency in a free election. *NIGERIA:* Biafra's struggle for independence left two million dead and millions more facing starvation. *SINAI:* On August 7, Egypt and Israel signed a 90-day cease fire along the Suez Canal. The following month, Nasser died suddenly and Anwar Sadat, 52, succeeded him as president, pledging "to continue the struggle for liberation of Arab lands." *JORDAN:* A civil war broke out with Palestinian guerillas; invading Syrian tanks were beaten back by King Hussein's air force. Arab commandos highjacked four western airliners precipitating a world crisis. Forced to land near Aman (and one at Cairo) they were blown up only minutes after the passengers were released.

EAST PAKISTAN: A cyclone devastated the coast in one of the worst disasters of modern times. *FRANCE:* Premier Pompidou agreed to sell 100 Mirages to Libya. *CANADA:* Premier Trudeau declared a war emergency after Quebec Liberation terrorists kidnapped officials and murdered Labor Minister Laporte.

DEATHS: Charles de Gaulle, Walter Reuther, Bertrand Russell, Mark Rothko, Rube Goldberg, Vince Lombardi, Janis Joplin, Gypsy Rose Lee.

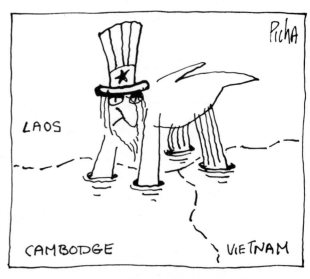

JEAN-PAUL WALRAVENS (PICHA)/*Belgium*

BILL MAULDIN/*Chicago Sun-Times*

'Peace' is when nobody's shooting. A 'just peace' is when our side gets what it wants.

KENNETH MAHOOD/*Punch, London*

BERNARD HANDELSMAN/*Punch, London*

DOONESBURY

GARY TRUDEAU/*Universal Press Syndicate*

FEIFFER

I PUSH THE FIRST BUTTON.

AN AMERICAN ARMY, UN-DEFEATED IN THE FIELD OF BATTLE, WILL COME HOME IN HUMILIATION—

I PUSH THE SECOND BUTTON.

BECAUSE IMPATIENT PACIFISTS IN THE SENATE LOST THE WAR.

I PUSH THE THIRD BUTTON.

ARE THE ISOLATIONISTS CONTENT TO LET ASIA GO BY DEFAULT TO THE COMMUNISTS?

I PUSH THE FOURTH BUTTON.

WHILE I DO NOT QUESTION THEIR PATRIOTISM—

I PUSH THE FIFTH BUTTON.

TWENTY YEARS OF TREASON!

OOPS— WRONG BUTTON.

Dist. Publishers-Hall Syndicate

JULES FEIFFER/ *Field Newspaper Syndicate*

FINN GRAFF 70

FINN GRAFF/ *Arbeiderbladet, Norway*

HIS MASTER'S VOICE

ABU/*Delhi Express, India*

LEST WE FORGET

DANIEL AGUILA/*Filipino Reporter*

CORKY TRINIDAD/*Los Angeles Times*

I'm sure worried about my brother. He goes to a university back home.

DAVID LEVINE/*New York Review of Books*

POGO

WALT KELLY/*Publishers-Hall Syndicate*

CESAR CHAVEZ FARM WORKERS' STRIKE

BRAD HOLLAND/ *New York Times*

MOISHE DAYAN

ALI BABA AND THE FORTY THIEVES

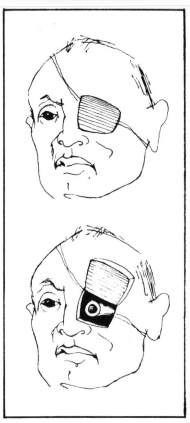

JEAN-PAUL WALRAVENS (PICHA)/*Belgium*

АЛИ-БАБА И СОРОК РАЗБОЙНИКОВ

Рисунок Е. ШУКАЕВА

E. SHUKAYER/*Krokodil, U.S.S.R.*

HORST/*Nebelspalter, Switzerland*

If the Israelis weren't such spoil-sports we could fight the whole Near East war abroad.

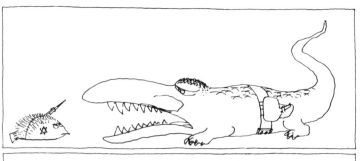

GUSTAV PEICHL (IRONIMUS)/*Die Presse, Austria*

MADAME DE POMPIDOU

ROY PETERSON/_Vancouver Sun, Canada_

BRANDT NEW EAGLE

MERLE TINGLEY (TING)/_London Free Press, Canada_

PIERRE BELLOCQ/ _Philadelphia Inquirer_

Above all, enjoy your meal . . .

JAN BAKKER/*Rotterdam-Zuid, Holland*

BIAFRA

WITH FEELINGS OF DEEPEST SYMPATHY

FRITZ BEHRENDT/*Het Brool, Holland*

ENRIQUE MEDAL/*La Provincia , Spain*

JANUSZ MAJEWSKI (MAYK)/*Sydsvenska Dagbladet, Sweden*

Goldberg is the name—Rube Goldberg.

KARL HUBENTHAL/*Los Angeles Herald-Examiner*

JÓZSEF SZÜR-SZABÓ/*Ludas Matyi, Hungary*

AT THE MOUTH OF THE GANGES

JIM DOBBINS/*Boston Herald-Examiner*

1971

SOUTHEAST ASIA: The United States entered the second decade of its involvement in the Vietnam War. Fighting was sporadic, reflecting the "Vietnamization" plan, as the South Vietnamese forces assumed a greater ground combat role. However, between December 26 and 30, 200 U.S. planes attacked North Vietnam in the heaviest bombing of the war. *PROTESTS:* Nationwide demonstrations flared against the prolonged U.S. involvement in Vietnam. Police dispersed 200,000 people encamped in Washington D.C. parks and made over 10,000 arrests.

CHINA: The People's Republic was seated in the UN, and Nationalist China (Taiwan) expelled. A touring U.S. table tennis team was greeted by Premier Chou En-lai. *RUSSIA:* Nine Soviet Jews were sentenced to prison for anti-Soviet actions. *PARIS:* Vietnam peace talks remained thoroughly snarled. *ENGLAND:* Membership in the Common Market approved—a major victory for Prime Minister Edward Heath. *MID-EAST:* Anwar Sadat called 1971 the decisive year of war or peace with Israel. Golda Meir rejected a U.S. proposal to open the Suez Canal giving Egypt control of the Canal's both banks.

PENTAGON PAPERS: The New York Times published a sensational series of articles based on a top-secret study of Vietnam policy suppied by former Pentagon analyst, Daniel Ellsberg. *SUPREME COURT:* The government's attempt at "prior restraint" to prevent publication of the Pentagon Papers was denied. The Senate confirmed Lewis Powell and William Rehnquist, who joined the two other Nixon appointees, Chief Justice Burger and Harry Blackmun, to form a "strict constructionist bloc." *TRIALS:* Lt. William Calley, Jr., was found guilty of murdering twenty-two civilians at My Lai in South Vietnam in 1968.

ECONOMY: In a dramatic turnabout President Nixon instituted Phase I, a ninety-day freeze on prices and wages, followed by Phase II, establishing economic control boards. *DESEGREGATION:* Alabama Governor George Wallace continued efforts to thwart court busing orders. *FBI:* J. Edgar Hoover was assailed for wiretapping and snooping on Capitol Hill. *GEORGIA:* Jimmy Carter was sworn in as Governor.

HEADLINES: General Motors recalled 6.7 million cars for defects. Guards stormed New York's Attica Prison on orders of Governor Rockefeller, ending a five-day uprising, leaving thirty-two prisoners and ten hostages dead. *SPACE:* The U. S. completed two successful moon missions, Apollo 14 and 15. *BUSINESS:* A $250-million government-guaranteed loan saved Lockheed Aircraft Corporation from bankruptcy.

DEATHS: Dean Acheson, Thomas E. Dewey, Hugo Black, Nikita Krushchev, Louis Armstrong, Ralph Bunche, Bobby Jones, Harold Lloyd, Igor Stravinsky, Ogden Nash, David Sarnoff.

ATTICA 71

BILL SANDERS/*Milwaukee Journal*

THE MILWAUKEE JOURNAL
TM ® All rights reserved 1971
Publishers-Hall Syndicate

. . . for his supporting role in 'Calley, The National Hero.'

WALLY FAWKES (TROG)/*Punch, London*

*I won them all in Vietnam
except this one which I got
for getting out of Vietnam.*

KENNETH MAHOOD/*Punch, London*

Time to come out of hiding . . .?

EWERT KARLSSON (EWK)/Aftonbladet, Sweden

DUNCAN MacPHERSON/ Toronto Star

TIN SANG/ South Vietnam

Bring in the defendant, Dr. Daniel Ellsberg.

DAVID LEVINE/*New York Review of Books*

FEIFFER

JULES FEIFFER/*Field Newspaper Syndicate*

PETER ALDOR/*El Tiempo, Colombia*

The other Lincoln: "Will he succeed in extinguishing the opposition's enthusiasm?"

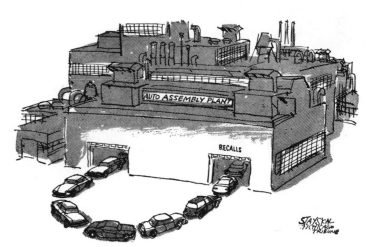

WAYNE STAYSKAL/*Chicago Tribune*

POGO

WALT KELLY/*Publishers-Hall Syndicate*

WALLY FAWKES (TROG)/ *Punch, London*

CHRISTINE LANIEL/*Canada*

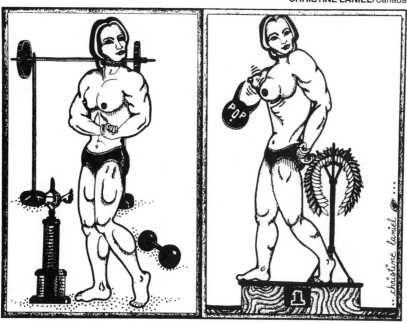

POGO

WALT KELLY/*Publishers-Hall Syndicate*

PRECISION DANCING

GENE BASSET/*Scripps-Howard Newspapers*

JIM BERRY/ *Newspaper Enterprise Association*

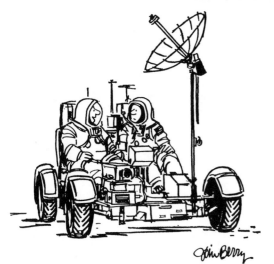

Think of it! We're the first men on Earth ever to drive a $13-million car!

From out there, it all looks good.   **VIC RUNTZ**/ *Bangor Daily News*

HIROSHI OOBA/*Japan*

SHEMUEL KATZ (SHMULIK)/*Al-Hamishmar, Israel*

FRANCE'S MOST IMPORTANT CHANGE

MOISAN/*Le Canard Enchaine, Paris*

WALLY FAWKES (TROG)/*Punch, London*

Come on—it may not be too late!

MY POUND IS MY CASTLE

JAN O. HENRIKSEN (JANO)
Faedrelandsvennen, Norway

DON WRIGHT/*Miami News*

China's membership in the United Nations: a new seating plan?

VIAKAL/*Hindu Weekly Review, India*

*And assure him, we will recognize the government in Washington
as the legitimate government of the United States.*

GERMAN MALVIDO O'CADIZ
El Universal, Mexico

LET MY PEOPLE GO

EUGENE MIHAESCO/*New York Times*

REQUIEM FOR JAZZ

HERC FICKLEN/_Dallas Morning News_

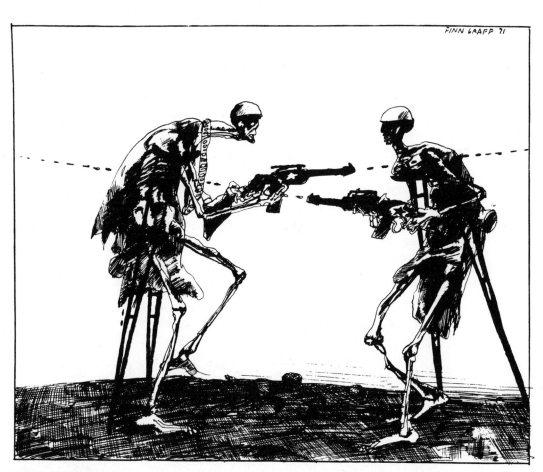

INDIA-PAKISTAN

FINN GRAFF/_Arbeiderbladet, Norway_

1972

CAMPAIGN: After losses in Pennsylvania and Massachusetts, Senator Edmund Muskie withdrew from the presidential race. Senator George McGovern's fervid grass roots support carried him to the Democratic nomination. When it was disclosed that his running mate Tom Eagleton had undergone psychiatric treatment, he was dropped from the ticket, irreversibly damaging the McGovern candidacy. For the first time, the AFL-CIO, led by George Meany, refused to back the Democratic ticket. A would-be assassin, Arthur Bremer, shot and partially paralyzed George Wallace during a Maryland primary rally, forcing the governor's withdrawal from the race. ELECTION: In the lowest voter turnout in 24 years, Nixon and Agnew were easy victors over McGovern and his new running mate, Sargent Shriver.

WATERGATE: On June 17, five men were caught bugging the Democratic National Headquarters in Washington D. C.'s Watergate complex, which press secretary Ron Ziegler downplayed as a "third-rate burglary." Despite evidence of links to Nixon's White House and re-election campaign, the dimensions of the scandal were not perceived in time to influence the election.

VIOLENCE: Palestinian terrorists took the Israeli wrestling team hostage at the Munich Summer Olympics; eleven athletes were massacred. SKY-JACKING: A new world-wide phenomenon, twentieth-century air piracy. Ransomers, terrorists, political dissidents, and common criminals commandeered scores of aircraft, flying many of them to Cuba. CONFLICTS: The blood-letting continued in North Ireland between Catholics and Protestants. In Rhodesia the black minority moved towards civil war in angry reaction against British sanctioning of a white-supremacist regime.

SUMMITS: President Nixon made an historic trip to the People's Republic of China. The former cold warrior toasted the beginning of "a long march together" with Premier Chairman Mao Tse-tung and Vice Premier Chou En-lai. Despite America's massive bombing and the mining of North Vietnamese ports, Nixon met in Moscow with Brezhnev and signed the first SALT agreement.

PARIS: Henry Kissinger continued his on-and-off-again peace talks with North Vietnam's Le Duc Tho. CAIRO: President Sadat invited Russia out of Egypt.

DOMESTIC NEWS: The Supreme Court ruled that journalists must reveal confidential sources and information to grand juries. Drug addiction reached epidemic proportions in the United States and among the armed forces in Vietnam. Soaring U. S. grain prices resulted from massive purchases by the Soviet Union. Clifford Iriving was indicted for the bogus Howard Hughes memoirs caper. Bobby Fisher defeated Boris Spassky for the world chess title in Iceland. The Senate approved the Equal Rights Amendment. The Surgeon General warned that cigarette smoke is also a danger to the non-smoker.

DEATHS: Harry S Truman, J. Edgar Hoover, the Duke of Windsor (former Edward VIII of England), Adam Clayton Powell, Jr., Walter Winchell, Jackie Robinson.

LOUIS MITLBERG (TIM)/*Paris-Match, France*

NIXON GOES TO CHINA

MIKE PETERS/*Dayton Daily News*

NIXON IN PEKING

GUSTAV PEICHL (IRONIMUS)/*Die Presse, Austria*

BOB HOWIE/*Jackson Daily News*

BEN WICKS/*Toronto Telegram, Canada*

DUNCAN MacPHERSON/*Toronto Star, Canada*

Stop doing that to your eyes Dick and come to bed!

1972

DAVID LEVINE/*New York Review of Books*

PAT OLIPHANT/*Washington Star*

All I ever get is tea—why is that, Kissinger?

JIM BERRY/*Newspaper Enterprise Association*

You will meet a stunningly attractive girl and escort her to a party—Henry, I think I got your fortune cookie!

BILL SANDERS/*Milwaukee Journal*

THE MILWAUKEE JOURNAL

*We must not falter. For all that we have risked and all that
we have gained over the years now hangs in the balance . . .*

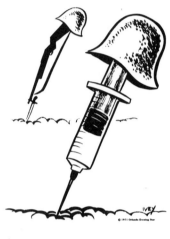

JIM IVY/*Orlando Sentinel*

THE SOUTH VIETNAMESE HAVE MADE GREAT PROGRESS. THEY ARE NOW BEARING THE BRUNT OF THE BATTLE. AND WE CAN NOW SEE THE DAY..

WHEN NO MORE AMERICANS WILL BE INVOLVED THERE AT ALL. AND THAT IS WHY I SAY TO YOU TONIGHT..

© 1972 JULES FEIFFER 6-4

LET US END THE WAR. BUT LET US END IT IN SUCH A WAY THAT THE YOUNGER BROTHERS AND SONS OF THE BRAVE MEN WHO HAVE FOUGHT..

WILL NOT HAVE TO FIGHT AGAIN IN SOME OTHER VIETNAM AT SOME TIME IN THE FUTURE.

Dist. Publishers-Hall Syndicate

FEIFFER

JULES FEIFFER/*Field Newspaper Syndicate*

1972

SUAR/*Tio Landry, Mexico City*

ENDANGERED SPECIES

TOM DARCY/*Long Island Newsday*

'Greetings, French Liberators!'

'Greetings, Nationalist Liberators!'

'Greetings, Viet Cong Liberators!'

'Greetings, American Liberators!'

'Greetings, Government Liberators!'

'Greetings, North Vietnamese Liberators!'

GREETINGS, B-52s...

PAT OLIPHANT/*Washington Star*

WITHDRAWAL

DOONESBURY

LOU MYERS/*Politicks Magazine*

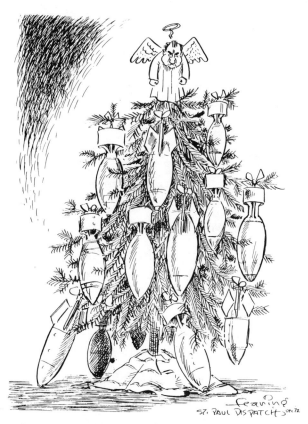

JERRY FEARING/*St. Paul Dispatch*

EDMUND VALTMAN/*Hartford Times*

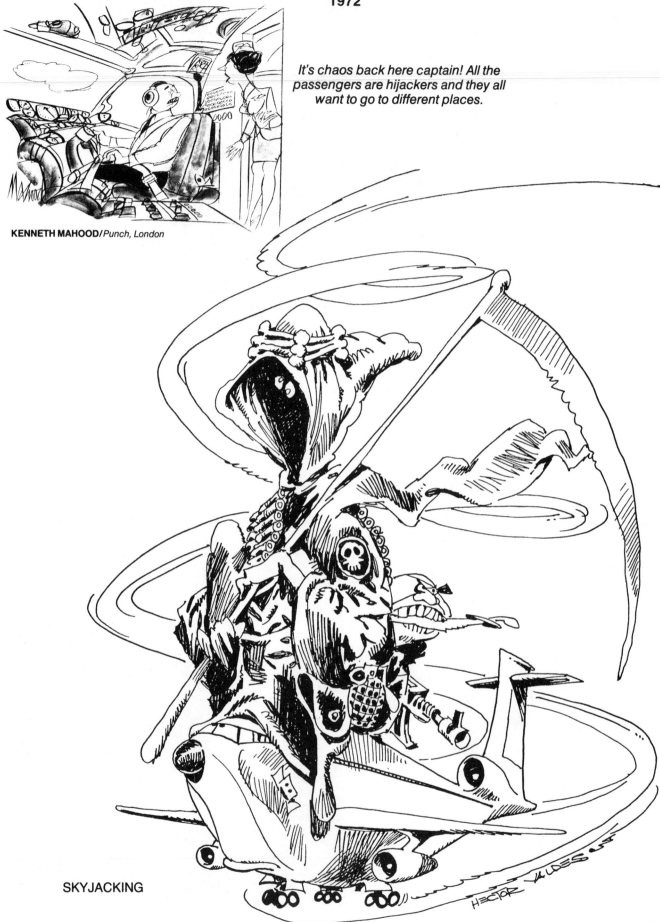

It's chaos back here captain! All the passengers are hijackers and they all want to go to different places.

KENNETH MAHOOD/*Punch, London*

SKYJACKING

HECTOR VALDES/*El Heraldo de Mexico, Mexico City*

OLYMPIC DREAM
FRITZ BEHRENDT/*Het Brool, Holland*

YET ANOTHER RAID TO THE NORTH

TERRY MOSHER (AISLIN)/*Montreal Gazette, Canada*

DON MOORE/*WGN-TV, Chicago*

BLACK SEPTEMBER

DUNCAN MacPHERSON/*Toronto Star, Canada*

THE LONDON-SALISBURY DEAL

BORIS EFIMOV/*Izvestiya, Moscow*

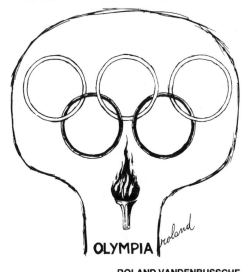

ROLAND VANDENBUSSCHE
Gazet Van Antwerpen, Belgium

ABE BERRY/*The Star, South Africa*

VADILLO/ *Siempre!, Mexico City*

EDUARDO DEL RIO (RUIS)/*Proceso, Mexico*

TONY AUTH/*Philadelphia Inquirer*

CHARLES BISSELL/ *Nashville Tennessean*

BOBBY FISCHER

TERRY MOSHER (AISLIN)/ *Montreal Gazette Canada*

JACK DAVIS/ *Time Magazine*

GUSTAV PEICHL (IRONIMUS)/ *Die Presse, Austria*

A DANCE TO '72.

IN THIS DANCE I CELEBRATE THE OLD-FASHIONED AMERICAN VIRTUE OF—

Dist. Publishers-Hall Syndicate

WINNING!

WINNING THE WAR AGAINST VIETNAM.

WINNING THE WAR AGAINST THE ECONOMY.

WINNING THE WAR AGAINST THE DEMOCRATS.

WINNING THE WAR AGAINST...

MYSELF.

© 1972 JULES FEIFFER 1-9

FEIFFER

JULES FEIFFER/ *Field Newspaper Syndicate*

TOM CURTIS/ *Milwaukee Sentinel*

CHARLES BROOKS, *Birmingham News*

You blasted idiot! I keep telling you I'm feeling fine!

CHARLES SAXON/ *The New Yorker*

I want you to promise me you'll give McGovern one more chance to turn you on.

THE OLD BOMBER PILOT

DON WRIGHT/*Miami News*

STEVE MILLER/*Honolulu Star-Bulletin*

NIXON'S "NEW MAJORITY"

BOB ZSCHIESCHE/*Greensboro News*

What, Me Worry?

Coo-o-o.

TOM ENGLEHART
St. Louis Post-Dispatch

CARL LARSEN/*Richmond Times-Dispatch*

Congratulations, Mr. Shriver.

TONY AUTH/*Philadelphia Inquirer*

TOM CURTIS/*Milwaukee Sentinel*

JACK BENDER/*Waterloo Courier*

RUNNING FOR THE PRESIDENCY—1972

JIM DOBBINS/*Boston Herald-Examiner*

TONY AUTH/*Philadelphia Inquirer*

AUTH

WATERGATE INVESTIGATION

JUSTICE DEPT.

JUSTICE DEPT.

Thou mayest announce to the assembled multitudes that my governmental reorganization is complete.

Richard the I

HUGH HAYNIE/*Louisville Courier-Journal*

ROY PETERSON/*Vancouver Sun, Canada*

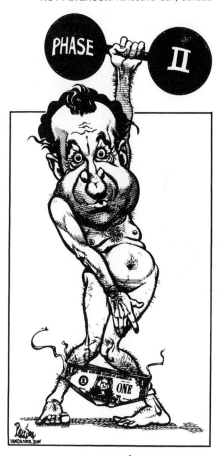

. . . oops!

IVAN TODOROV/Bulgaria

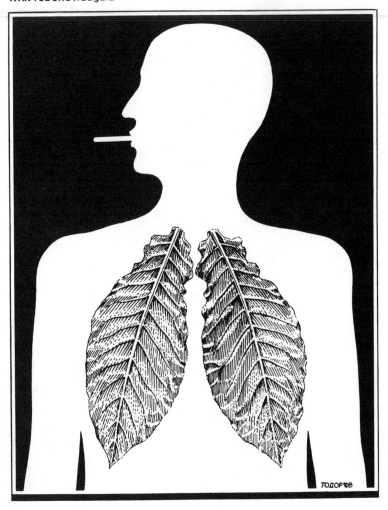

ANONYMOUS/Krokodil Magazine, U.S.S.R.

COVER OF ANTI-SMOKING ISSUE

WAYNE STAYSKAL/Chicago Tribune

This isn't so bad, considering some companies have banned smoking areas altogether!

BILL MAULDIN/ *Chicago Sun-Times*

CHIP BOK/ *Kettering Oakwood Times*

BOB ZSCHIESCHE/ *Greensboro News*

THE MAN FROM INDEPENDENCE

We were good friends.

FRANK WILLIAMS/ *Detroit Free Press*

Global Concerns I

In addition to the day-to-day news in the 1970's, cartoonists dealt with a number of continuing and growing human concerns. Cartoonists from various countries and cultures, of all political, social, and philosophical persuasions found common enemies in pollution, war, hunger, crime, urbanization, and population growth—and vigorously attacked them employing a diverse vocabulary of graphics and humor. This section deals with some of the many problems of pollution of the environment—air, water, and natural resources. A selection of cartoons concerned with war, crime, urbanization, obsessive technology, and over-population appears on pages 140 to 145.

FUN CITY

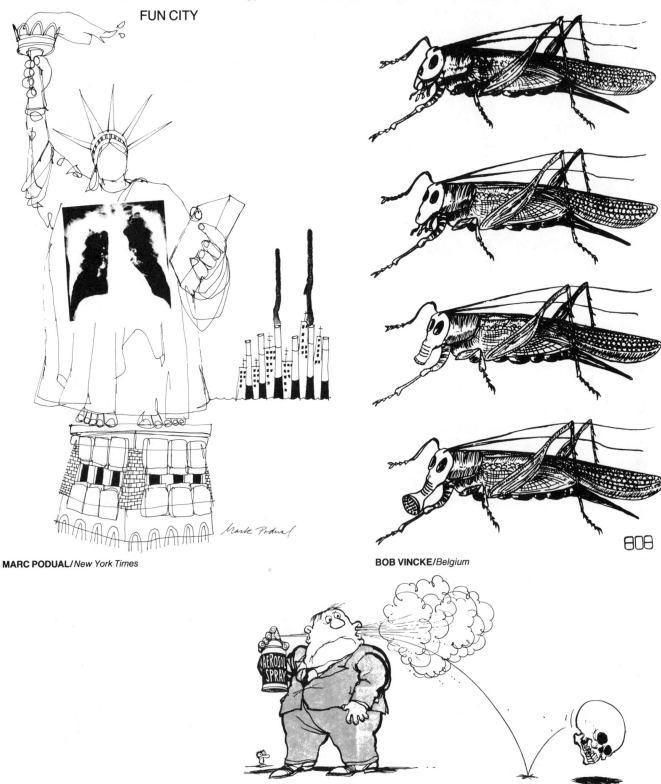

MARC PODUAL/*New York Times*

BOB VINCKE/*Belgium*

PAT OLIPHANT/*Washington Star*

THE FIFTH HORSEMAN OF THE APOCALYPSE   **EDWARD McLACHLAN/***Punch, London*

Little Poppleford? It's in there somewhere.   **MICHAEL FFOLKES/***Punch, London*

WILLIAM SCULLY/*Punch, London*

*It isn't anything like as bad as it was—a little
while ago you couldn't see the bedsteads.*

DOUGLAS FLORIAN
The New Yorker

The air quality certainly looks 'unhealthy' today.

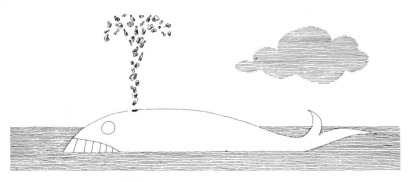

JHON KRIAKOPOULOS (KUP)/*Greece*

JERRY FLISAK/*Poland*

SILENT SPRING

L. D. WARREN/*Cincinnati Enquirer*

MARTIAL LEITER/_La Tuile, Switzerland_

PHOTO D'ENTREPRISE

DENNIS RENAULT/ *Sacramento Bee*

TERRY MOSHER (AISLIN)/ *Montreal Gazette*

PESTICYCLE

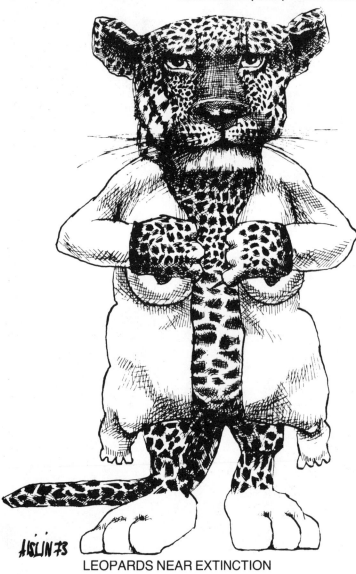

AISLIN 73

LEOPARDS NEAR EXTINCTION

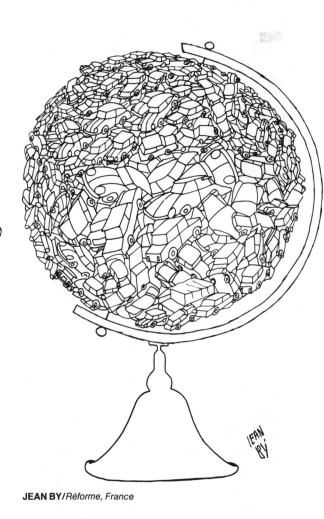

JEAN BY/ *Réforme, France*

Global Concerns

COR HOEKSTRA (CORK)/*Natuur & Landschap, The Netherlands*

RASIT YAKALI/*Pardon Mizah Dergisi, Turkey*

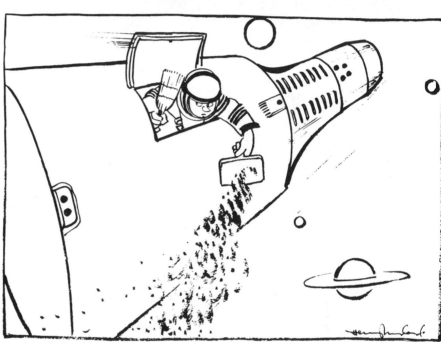

HENRY IMSLAND/ *Stavanger Aftenblad, Norway*

MOISAN/*Le Canard Enchaine, Paris*

Ah, you've been in for a swim?

CARLOS J. VILAR ALEMAN/*Dedete, Cuba*

KLAUS VONDERWERTH/*Veband-Bildender Kunstler, E. Germany*

ANONYMOUS/*Krokodil Magazine, U.S.S.R.*

CHARLES E. MARTIN (CEM)/*The New Yorker*

EUGEN TARU/*Urzica, Roumania*

ANTONIO MELE (MELANTON)/*Italy*

THE PUBLI-CITY

JERRY FLISAK/*Poland*

60

OTO REISENGER/ *Vjesnik, Jugolsavia*

No! This time you're going to try it without people.

HANS MOSER/ *Nebelspalter, Switzerland*

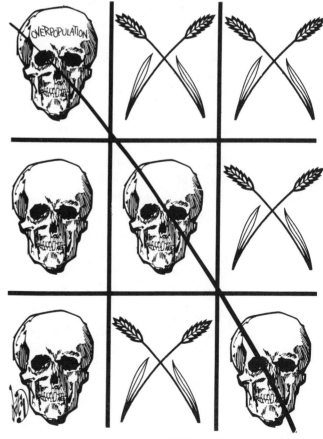

TOM DARCY/ *Long Island Newsday*

1973

WATERGATE: Defendant James McCord wrote an explosive letter to Judge John Sirica charging that perjury by the Watergate burglars concealed high-level guilt. John Dean, former Nixon counsel, testified before the Select Senate Committee, headed by folksy Senator Sam Ervin of North Carolina, that President Nixon was a conspirator in the cover-up. Wholesale resignations of the Nixon staff followed, including H. R. Haldeman and John Ehrlichman. Dean was fired. *TAPES:* White House aide Alexander Butterfield's testimony was shocking—secret tape recordings were made of all conversations in the Oval Office during the Watergate period. Nixon's desperate efforts to keep the subpoenaed tapes secret resulted in the "Saturday Night Massacre": the resignation of Attorney General Elliot Richardson, his deputy, William Ruckleshaus, and the firing of Special Prosecutor Archibald Cox. The public outrage and threats of impeachment compelled the release of some tapes. One contained a mysterious 18-minute gap, which the White House claimed was accidentally erased by Nixon's secretary, Rose Mary Woods. The beleagured president was defiant: "I am not a crook!"

SPIRO AGNEW: The Vice President, faced with charges of bribery and extortion, resigned and was convicted of tax evasion. Gerald Ford replaced him as Vice President.

SPENDING: Other investigations centered on the estimated $10 million spent on Nixon residences in San Clemente and Key Biscayne and over $50 million raised for Nixon's re-election.

YOM KIPPUR WAR: Israel was surprised by Egypt with a lightning strike across the Suez Canal, their fourth war in twenty-five years. *INDOCHINA:* North Vietnam and the U.S. finally signed a peace agreement on January 23 and the American troops began to withdraw after the longest war in its history. *SOUTH AMERICA:* Marxist president Salvador Allende Gossens of Chile was murdered by a rightist military junta, headed by General Augusto Pinochet Ugarte, unleashing a reign of terror. Exiled Juan Peron returned to power in Argentina. *GREECE:* The military regime of General Papadopoulos was overthrown by Brig. Demetrius Zoannites in a rightist coup.

ENERGY: The Arab states retaliated for U.S. support of Israel with an oil embargo. Motorists endured high prices, short supply and long gas lines. Congress approved construction of a $3.5-billion, 789 mile oil pipeline across Alaskan frozen wilderness.

NUMBERS: Apollo astronauts successfully docked with Sky Lab I, repairing the damaged space station. Sky Lab II astronauts spent 59 days orbiting the earth. At year's end, Sky Lab III was launched, attempting a new endurance record. Economic Control phases III and IV failed to produce results. *PROTEST:* American Indians staged an uprising at Wounded Knee in South Dakota citing numerous violations of federal treaties and denial of tribal rights.

DEATHS: Lyndon Baines Johnson, David Ben-Gurion, Pablo Casals, Pablo Picasso, Edward Steichen, Pearl Buck, John Ford, Eddie Rickenbacker.

DAVID LEVINE/*New York Review of Books*

THE OUTRAGE OF WIRETAPS

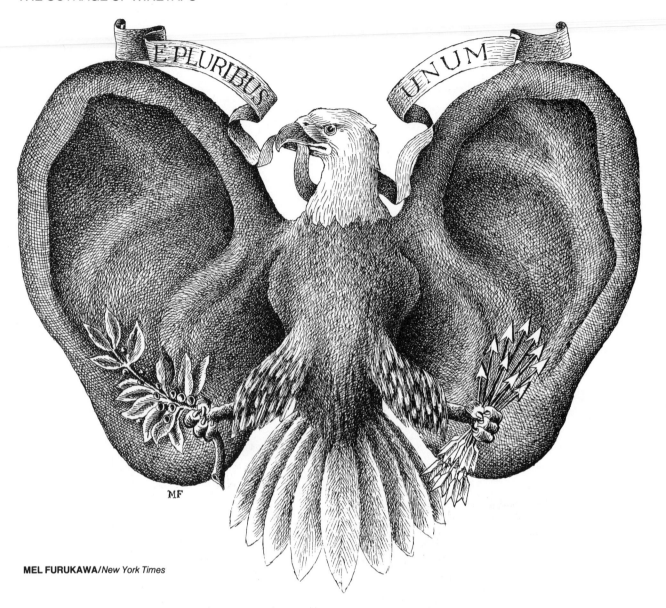

MEL FURUKAWA/_New York Times_

DOONESBURY

GARY TRUDEAU/ _Universal Press Syndicate_

RON, DOES THE PRESIDENT HAVE ANY COMMENT ON THE MOST RECENT DISCLOSURES IN THE WATERGATE CASE!

NO!

WATERGATE! WATERGATE! WHAT IS THE MATTER WITH YOU GUYS?! WHAT IS THIS **SENSELESS** ORGY OF RECRIMINATION WEEK AFTER WEEK?!

I'VE ALREADY SAID ALL THAT I'M GOING TO! SO WHY DON'T YOU STOP WASTING BOTH OUR TIME AND ASK ME QUESTIONS I CAN DEAL WITH?

RON, WHAT COLOR SHIRT IS THE PRESIDENT WEARING TODAY?

THAT'S BETTER. BLUE.

THE SPIDER WEB

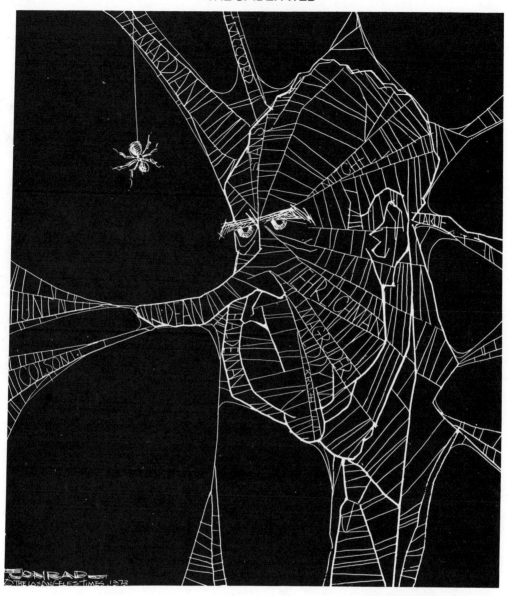

PAUL CONRAD/*Los Angeles Times*

DOONESBURY

GARY TRUDEAU/ *Universal Press Syndicate*

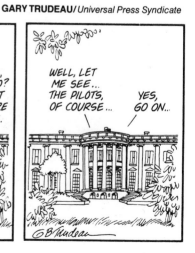

Ouch!

DON HESSE/St. Louis Globe-Democrat

I claim executive privilege.

AUTH

TONY AUTH/Philadelphia Inquirer

I WANT **YOUR** TAPES
FOR THE SENATE WATERGATE COMMITTEE

ROBERT GRAYSMITH/ *San Francisco Chronicle*

FRITZ BEHRENDT/ *Het Brool, Holland*

JEFF MacNELLY/ *Richmond News-Leader*

INSIDE H. R. HALDEMAN

HELLO BLEEP
THIS IS
YOUR BLEEP
PRESIDENT
SPEAKING...

PAT OLIPHANT/*Washington Star*

STILL LIFE

I hear Ehrlichman and Haldeman went to college together.

...and they both made the Dean's list!

JERRY ROBINSON/*Cartoonists & Writers Syndicate*

NIXON'S THE ONE

PAUL SZEP/*Boston Globe*

PAT OLIPHANT/*Washington Star*

We were only obeying orders! . . .

BILL SANDERS/*Milwaukee Journal*

BELOW OLYMPUS

FRANK INTERLANDI/*Los Angeles Times*

*Now let's go over that part again, Alice, where
you slipped and fell into the rabbit hole.*

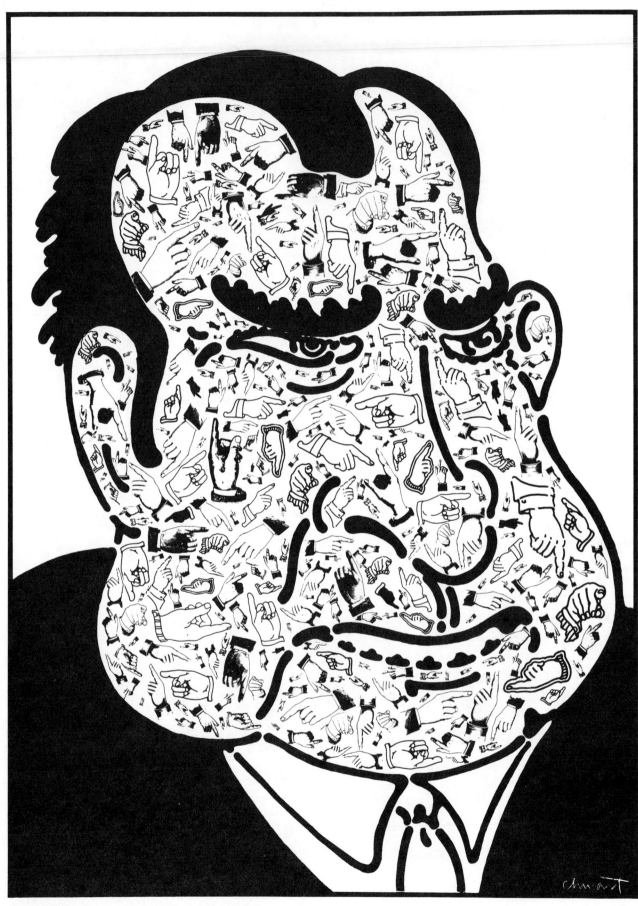

SEYMOUR CHWAST/_New York Times_

RICHARD HESS/ *New York Magazine*

THE MISSING TAPES

MIKE PETERS/ *Dayton Daily News*

1973

A CODE OF LOYALTY

R. O. BLECKMAN/*New York Times*

VANDALISM

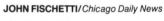

ROY JUSTUS/*Minneapolis Star*

JOHN FISCHETTI/*Chicago Daily News*

Will the last one indicted please put the lights out?

DAVID LEVINE/New York Review of Books

THIS IS DAN RATHER AT SAN CLEMENTE, A.K.A. "THE WESTERN WHITE HOUSE."

THE SUMMIT TALKS BETWEEN PRESIDENT NIXON AND SOVIET PARTY CHIEF BREZHNEV CONTINUED TODAY AS THE TWO LEADERS SAT OUTSIDE IN THE GARDENS OF THE CALIFORNIA ESTATE.

AT ONE POINT THIS AFTERNOON, MR. BREZHNEV TURNED TO HIS HOST AND INQUIRED WHEREVER DID HE FIND THE FUNDS TO FINANCE AND KEEP UP SUCH A LOVELY HOME!

IT WAS CONSIDERED BY MANY TO BE A LOW POINT IN THE TALKS.

DOONSEBURY

GARY TRUDEAU/Universal Press Syndicate

HELIOFLORES/ *El Universal, Mexico*

OH/ *El Correo Catalan, Spain*

GENE BASSET/ *Scripps-Howard Newspapers*

MILHOUS I

Lord of San Clemente
Duke of Key Biscayne
Captain of Watergate

JEFF MacNELLY/*Richmond News-Leader*

I know what you're probably thinking . . .

HUGH HAYNIE/*Louisville Courier-Journal*

. . . the whole truth and nothing but . . .

ROB LAWLOR/*Philadelphia Daily News*

RALPH STEADMAN/*Rolling Stone Magazine*

BACK VIEW

JURG SPAHR (JUSP)/*Bruckenbauer, Switzerland*

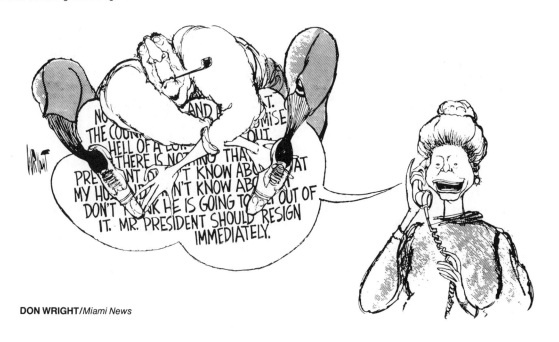

DON WRIGHT/*Miami News*

PAUL SZEP/ *Boston Globe*

*. . . keep remembering . . . health, a beautiful figure, and
no longer at the mercy of some Arab sheik with an oil well . . .*

LENARD NORRIS/ *Vancouver Sun, Canada*

THE ODD COUPLE

BILL MAULDIN/*Chicago Sun-Times*

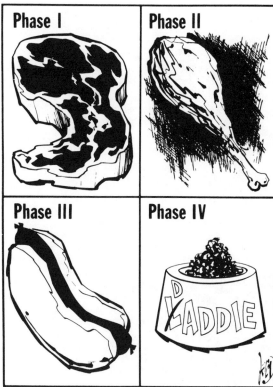

DON WRIGHT/*Miami News*

RACK UP ANOTHER ONE FOR BIG OIL.

JACK JURDEN/*Wilmington News Journal*

Phase I

Phase II

Phase III

Phase IV

TOM DARCY/*Long Island Newsday*

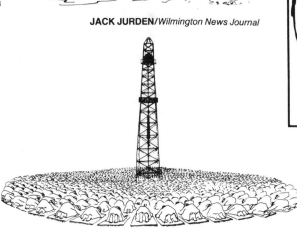

HERMAN VERCHAEREN/*Belgium*

PEACE TREATY SIGNED, VIETNAM

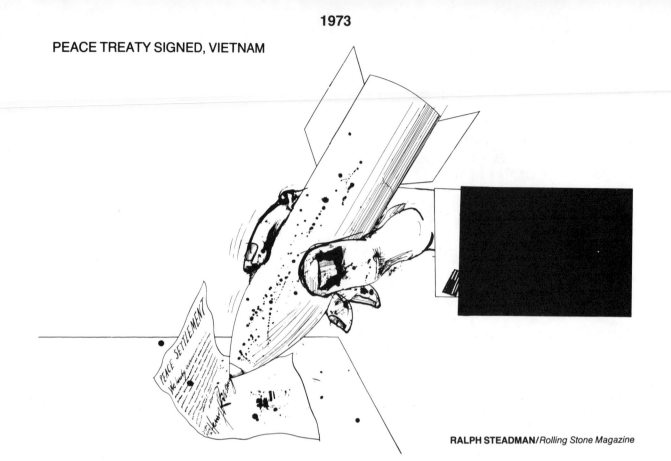

RALPH STEADMAN/*Rolling Stone Magazine*

TERRY MOSHER (AISLIN)/*Montreal Gazette*

ART PONIER/*Detroit News*

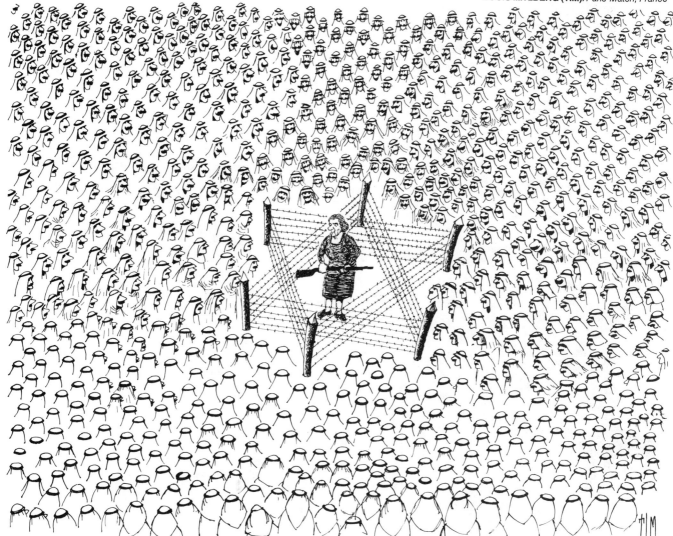

Smile! You are dancing because you are now a democracy!

ROGELIO NARANJO/*Actualidad, Mexico*

BILL PLYMPTON/*Soho Weekly News*

NGUYEN HAI CHI (CHOE)/*South Vietnam*

ROGELIO NARANJO/*Actualidad, Mexico*

PICASSO 73

PAUL SZEP/*Boston Globe*

'I WAS ALWAYS THANKFUL HE WASN'T A POLITICAL CARTOONIST!'

AT OLIPHANT/*Washington Star*

HERC FICKLEN/*Dallas Morning News*

1974

WATERGATE: The unfolding drama dominated the nation's consciousness—and conscience. Seven presidential aides, including John Mitchell, the nation's former chief law enforcement official, were indicted in March; the President, himself, was named as an unindicted co-conspirator. The scandal moved inexorably to its conclusion: May 9, the House Judiciary Committee began impeachment hearings; July 24, the Supreme Court unanimously ordered Nixon to yield up the subpoenaed White House tapes; July 27, the Committee voted the first of three Articles of Impeachment; August 5, the text of the "smoking gun" tape proved Nixon's involvement in the cover-up. Three days later, Nixon resigned in disgrace.

GERALD FORD: The new President promptly announced to an emotion-spent nation that, "Our long national nightmare is over." Less than a month later, Ford jarred the nation by granting Nixon a "full, free, and absolute pardon." Few responded to Ford's qualified amnesty for Vietnam deserters. Of the other Watergate accused, eighteen pleaded guilty, two were convicted, ten went to jail, and trials continued for five other principals.

SCANDAL: Wilbur Mills ended his long Congressional career after an alcoholic binge with his paramour, Fanne Foxe. ENERGY: The Arab oil embargo sent gasoline up to 60¢ a gallon and shock waves throughout the economy, exacerbating the deepest recession since the Great Depression. VIOLENCE, DISASTER & REPRESSION: Palestinian terrorists struck Maalot, killing 21 in the worst massacre in Israel's history. Heiress Patty Hearst, kidnapped by the

MacNELLY/THE RICHMOND NEWS LEADER ©1974 BY CHICAGO TRIBUNE

JEFF MacNELLY/*Richmond News-Leader*

Symbionese Liberation Army, was transformed into guerrilla "Tania". There was famine in Bangladesh and drought in Africa—700 million faced starvation worldwide. Portugal endured a revolution and a heavy toll in opposing liberation movements in its African colonies. A coup in Ethiopia overthrew venerable Emperor Haile Selassie. Alexander Solzhenitsyn, Nobel prize-winning author of *The Gulag Archipelago,* was exiled from the Soviet Union.

DIPLOMACY: The ubiquitous Henry Kissinger made nine trips in his shuttle diplomacy before truce agreements were finally signed establishing UN buffer zones along the Suez Canal and on the Golan Heights in Syria. President Ford, in pursuit of détente, signed the Vladivostok Agreement with Russia's Leonid Brezhnev, including a ceiling on ICBM and MIRV missiles.

OTHER HEADLINES; Evel Knievel failed in his Snake River Canyon jump; India detonated a nuclear bomb; Israeli Premier Golda Meir and West Germany's Chancellor Willy Brandt resigned; P.L.O. leader Arafat addressed the UN; Nelson Rockefeller became Vice President; violence broke out over school busing in Boston; political crises and terrorism flared in Cyprus, Italy, and North Ireland; and, in a barely noticed event, Jimmy Carter, a former one-term governor of Georgia, announced he was running for president of the U.S.

DEATHS: Georges Pompidou, Juan Peron, Earl Warren, Charles A. Lindbergh, H. L. Hunt, Samuel Goldwyn, Vittorio De Sica, Walter Lippmann, Duke Ellington, and Jack Benny.

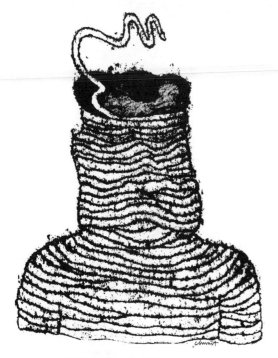

SEYMOUR CHWAST/*New York Times*

BILL GRAHAM/*Arkansas Gazette*

RONALD SEARLE
New York Times

ROBERT ENGLE/*Newsweek*

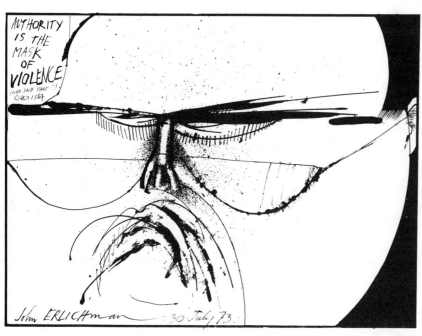

RALPH STEADMAN/*Rolling Stone Magazine*

DON WRIGHT/*Miami News*

DAVID LEVINE/New York Review of Books

BILL NELSON/New York Times

*I just wish the @**#%
transcriptions of the @**#%
tapes didn't have the word
'expletive' in it so @**#% often!*

JIM BERRY/Newspaper Enterprise Association

THE EXPULSION

ROBERT PRYOR/ *New York Times*

ROBERT GROSSMAN/ *New York Magazine*

ED SOREL/*New York Village Voice*   SYSYPHUS

FEIFFER   **JULES FEIFFER**/*Field Newspaper Syndicate*

BILL SCHORR/_Kansas City Star_

ROB LAWLOR/ _Philadelphia Daily News_

Hey guys, do you really think we need that clause about impeachment in there?

ROBERT GROSSMAN/_New York Magazine_

EDMUND VALTMAN/_Hartford Times_

BRAD HOLLAND/*New York Times*

THE AGE OF NIXON

JEAN-CLAUDE SUARES/*New York Times*

DAVID SUTER/*New York Times*

ROBERT GROSSMAN/*New York Magazine*

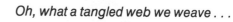
Oh, what a tangled web we weave . . .

CHARLES WERNER/*Indianapolis Star*

RALPH STEADMAN/*Rolling Stone Magazine*

I am not a crook . . . any more.

PAUL SZEP/ *Boston Globe*

ED SOREL/ *New York Magazine*

RALPH STEADMAN/ *Rolling Stone Magazine*

LOU MYERS/*Politicks Magazine*

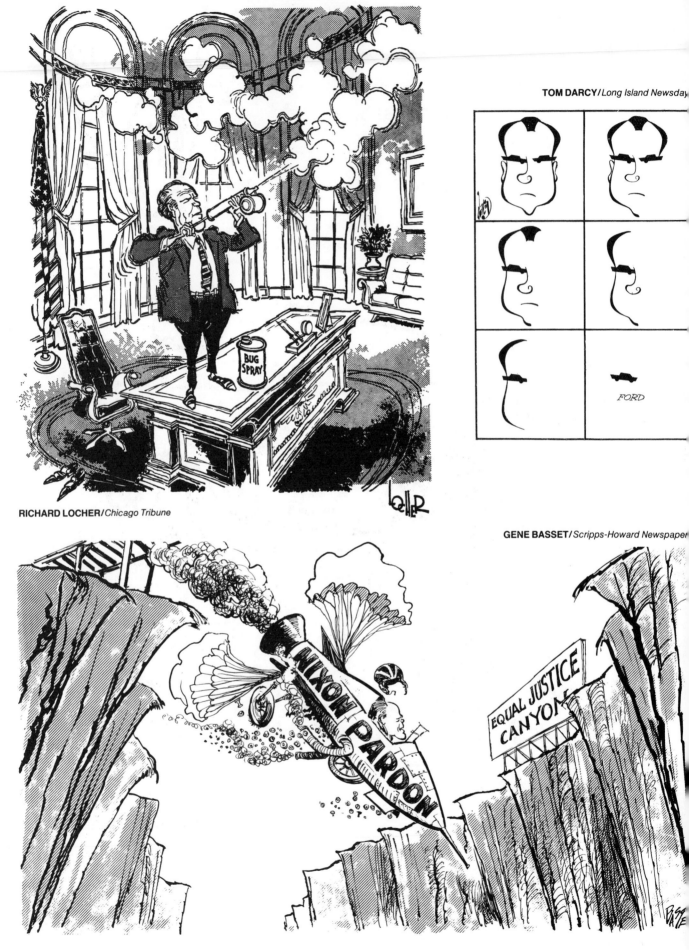

RICHARD LOCHER/*Chicago Tribune*

TOM DARCY/*Long Island Newsday*

FORD

GENE BASSET/*Scripps-Howard Newspaper*

NIXON PARDON

EQUAL JUSTICE CANYON

GENE BASSET/ *Scripps-Howard Newspapers*

We have a new game plan, men . . . WIN!

PAUL SZEP/ *Boston Globe*

DAVID LEVINE/New York Review of Books

ROBERT GROSSMAN/New York Magazine

OSWALDO SAGASTEGUI/*Excelsior, Mexico*

You're right . . . a Lincoln you ain't.

HUGH HAYNIE/*Louisville Courier-Journal*

SACRIFICE ON THE ALTAR

BOB TAYLOR/*Dallas Times Herald*

ROY PETERSON/*Vancouver Sun, Canada*

SANDY HUFFAKER/*New York Times*

JEFF MacNELLY/*Richmond News-Leader*

DETENTE

JACK DAVIS/*Time Magazine*

MICHA RICHTER/*The New Yorker*

"Détente."

UNITED NATIONS

"THEN IT'S UNANIMOUS....WE DEPLORE THE SENSELESS DEATHS OF THE THREE ARAB TERRORISTS.'

JEFF MacNELLY/*Richmond News-Leader*

...A cease fire resolution has been passed . . .
a cease fire resolution has been passed . . .
a cease fire . . .

KENNETH MAHOOD/*Punch, London*

LOUIS RAUWOLF/*Eulenspiegel, East Germany*

ROGELIO NARANJO/*Actualidad, Mexico*

JACK GOLD/*Kentucky Post*

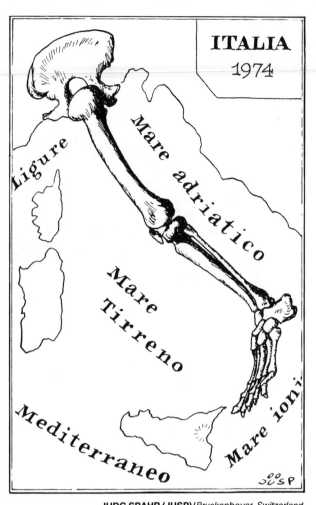

JURG SPAHR (JUSP)/*Bruckenbauer, Switzerland*

CRISE DU PETROLE

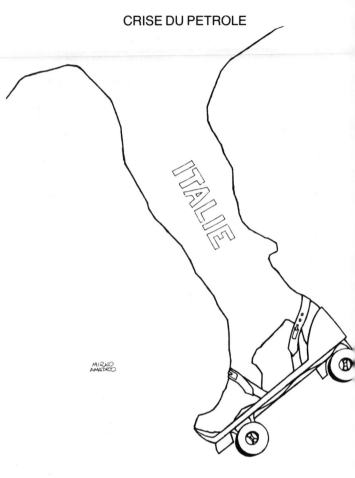

AMADEO MIRKO/*Candido*

—Be careful—he can still use his pen . . .

JAN O. HENRIKSEN (JANO)/*Faedrelandsvennen, Norway*

WALLY FAWKES (TROG)/ *Punch, London*

JOHN RIEDELL/ *Peoria Journal*

WHEN IRISH EYES AREN'T SMILING

L. D. WARREN/ *Cincinnati Enquirer*

PAT OLIPHANT/ *Denver Post*

ROGELIO NARANJO/ *Carteles y Portadas, Mexico*

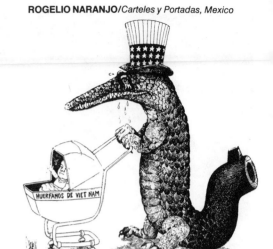

*It could be worse—we could be in Cyprus
trying to keep a bunch of Greeks and Turks apart!*

DUNCAN MacPHERSON/ *Toronto Star*

TICK . . . TOCK . . . TICK . . . TOCK . . . TICK . . . TOCK . . . TICK . . . TOCK . . . TICK . . . TOCK . . .

HERC FICKLEN/_Dallas Morning News_

ALOHA, LINDY

ALLENDE

BALTASAR DE ROSA/_Ahora, Uruguay_

Did you say 39?

DUKE ELLINGTON

KARL HUBENTHAL/_Los Angeles Herald-Examiner_

PAUL CONRAD/_Los Angeles Times_

1975

VIETNAM: The trauma finally came to a humiliating and graceless end for the United States as Americans and their Vietnamese employees madly scrambled aboard rescue helicopters atop the U.S. Embassy in Saigon. The undeclared war cost America 57,507 lives, 300,000 wounded, and $150 billion. MAYAGÜEZ: The United States endured still another tragedy in Southeast Asia when Cambodia's Khmer Rouge regime seized an American merchant ship. President Ford ordered a Marine rescue mission which liberated the ship and crew of 39, but at a cost of 38 U.S. dead and 50 wounded.

WATERGATE: The final chapter unfolded. H. R. Haldeman, John Ehrlichman, John Mitchell, and Robert Mardian were convicted of complicity in the cover-up. WOMEN & CRIME: Two assassination attempts on President Ford failed: Lynette "Squeaky" Fromme's gun didn't go off and Sarah Jane Moore's gun did, but Ford was unhurt. The FBI finally caught up with Patty Hearst and three other S.L.A. members. CIA & FBI: A wide pattern of CIA excesses, illegal conduct and worse was revealed, including domestic wire taps, burglaries, plots to assassinate foreign leaders, and testing drugs on unsuspecting victims. Sordid conduct by the FBI under J. Edgar Hoover was also disclosed, including vicious harrassment of Martin Luther King.

ECONOMY: Unemployment climbed to the highest since 1941, abetted by a 438% price increase by the oil cartel in two years. New York City faced bankruptcy. THE PRESIDENCY: Ford shook up his administration. Out:

Thanks a lot.

DON WRIGHT/*Miami News*

Secretary of Defense James Schlesinger, CIA Director William Colby, and Secretary of Commerce Rogers Morton. In: Donald Rumsfeld, George Bush, and Elliot Richardson. The President traveled to summit meetings in China and Europe, used his veto 32 times, and in November was challenged for his party's nomination by Ronald Reagan.

DEALS: Egypt and Israel came to a second-stage withdrawal agreement in the Sinai desert, midwifed by Henry Kissinger. The Soviet Union, finding its bread basket in the American west, contracted for 30 million metric tons of U.S. grain over the next five years. U.S.-U.S.S.R. détente reached a high point when Deke Slayton and Alexei Leonov linked up in space. *INDIA:* Indira Gandhi imposed a police state upon the world's most populous democracy, jailing hundreds of political enemies. *AFRICA:* Castro intervened in the Angola conflict. *UNITED NATIONS:* The General Assembly, supported by the Communist bloc and Third World nations, branded Zionism as "a form of racism". *NORTHERN IRELAND:* Bitter divisions continued between the Protestant majority and the Catholic minority.

ENTERTAINMENT: A Chorus Line was the toast of Broadway, and the film *Jaws,* a box office phenomenon, provided a new symbol for the nation's appreciative political cartoonists. (See Pages 114 and 182)

DEATHS: Chiang Kai-shek, Francisco Franco, Eamon deValera, King Faisal, Dimitri Shostakovich, Aristotle Onassis, Haile Selassie, Otto Soglow.

BRAD HOLLAND/ *New York Times*

A LESSON FOR THE SMALL STATE

IF YOU LIKED VIETNAM, YOU'LL LOVE THIS ONE!

ANGOLA

PRODUCED AND DIRECTED BY HENRY KISSINGER
STARRING THE C.I.A. AT A COST OF MILLIONS!

RATED
TOP SECRET

PAUL CONRAD/ *Los Angeles Times*

GUY BADEAUX (BADO)/ *Le Devoir, Canada*

ARE THERE TWO IRELANDS?

H. U. W.

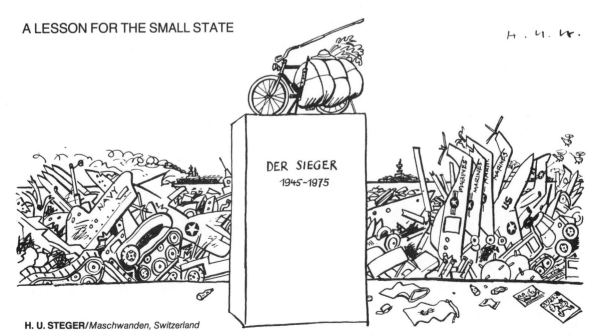

DER SIEGER
1945-1975

H. U. STEGER/ *Maschwanden, Switzerland*

Who said an elephant never forgets?

I am not a crook!

PAUL SZEP/ *Boston Globe*

VIC ROSCHKOV/ *Toronto Star, Canada*

TERRY MOSHER (AISLIN)/ *Montreal Gazette*

JEFF MacNELLY/*Richmond News-Leader*

SOVIET HARVEST

*Oh beautiful for spacious skies
For amber waves of grain . . .*

TONY AUTH/*Philadelphia Inquirer*

ED FISCHER/*Omaha World Herald*

TONY AUTH/Philadelphia Inquirer

The metamorphose of the PLO

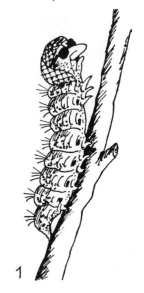

THE CANNIBALS

PAT OLIPHANT/Washington Star

OSWALDO SAGASTEGUI/Excelsior, Mexico

JURG SPAHR (JUSP)/Bruckenbauer, Switzerland

RICHARD LOCHER/*Chicago Tribune*

WARREN KING/*New York News* JAWS

DRAPER HILL/*Detroit News*

THE RECEPTION OF THE DIPLOMATIQUE & HIS SUITE AT THE COURT OF PEKING

PAUL SZEP/*Boston Globe*

ZE'EV/*Ha'aretz, Israel*

DON WRIGHT/*Miami News*

GOOD HOUSEKEEPING

THERE, IT'S **DONE**— MY CABINET COMPLETELY REORGANIZED, AND I DID IT ALL **MYSELF!**

—WAIT 'TIL I SHOW HENRY!

GOOD JOB, MR PRESIDENT! I LIKE THE WAY YOU HAVE ALL THE GOLF SHOES ON ONE SIDE AND THE SKI-BOOTS ON THE OTHER.

AND THE **WIN** BUTTONS ALL STACKED UP.

—AND YOUR SUITS ALL NEATLY LINED UP ON THEIR HANGERS—

YOU DESERVE A MEDAL!

—UH—WAIT A MINUTE MR PRESIDENT— I BELIEVE ONE OF THESE EMPTY SUITS IS ACTUALLY **DONALD H. RUMSFELD**

—YOU'RE RIGHT, HENRY— IT **IS** RUMSFELD! I'D BETTER FIX THAT.

WHY DON'T YOU MAKE HIM SECRETARY OF DEFENSE?

GOSH, HENRY WHAT WOULD I EVER DO WITHOUT YOU?

ROBERT GROSSMAN/*New York Magazine*

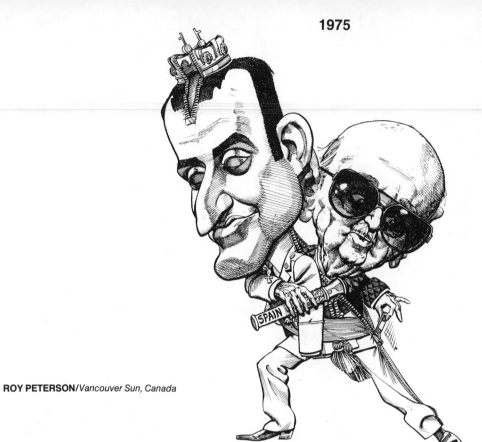

ROY PETERSON/Vancouver Sun, Canada

GENERAL FRANCISCO FRANCO
AND PRINCE JUAN CARLOS

BEFORE THE BIG TURN

H. U. STEGER/Maschwanden, Switzerland

FINN GRAFF/ Arbeiderbladet, Norway

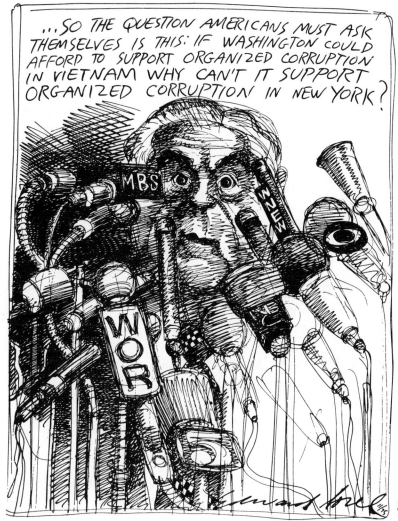

...SO THE QUESTION AMERICANS MUST ASK THEMSELVES IS THIS: IF WASHINGTON COULD AFFORD TO SUPPORT ORGANIZED CORRUPTION IN VIETNAM WHY CAN'T IT SUPPORT ORGANIZED CORRUPTION IN NEW YORK?

ED SOREL
New York Village Voice

New York City is still the big apple—Mayor Abe Beame

VERN THOMPSON/*Lawton Constitution Press*

ELDON PLETCHER/*New Orleans Times-Picayune*

117

GENE BASSET/ *Scripps-Howard Newspapers*

. . . and this one shows Mr. Hoover hot on the trail of Martin Luther King.

PAUL CONRAD/ *Los Angeles Times*

BIG THREE

MISSING

PATRICIA HEARST

MISSING

HOWARD HUGHES

MISSING

JAMES R. HOFFA

J. EDGAR HOOVER

JON KENNEDY/ *Arkansas Democrat*

. . . you have the right to remain silent . . .

DOUGLAS MARLETTE/*Charlotte Observer*

BILL SANDERS/*Milwaukee Journal*

STILL LIFE

you've been burglarized by the CIA, Tapped by the FBI, investigated by the IRS and under surveillance by the military...

I'm being Considered for a Job in the Civil Rights Division of the Justice Department!

JERRY ROBINSON/*Cartoonists & Writers Syndicate*

LOU MYERS/_Politicks Magazine_

DOUGLAS MARLETTE/_Charlotte Observer_

Where's it all going to end, O'Brien?

WAYNE STAYSKAL/_Chicago Tribune_

LODGE/_The Australian, Australia_

BILL MAULDIN/*Chicago Sun-Times*

Howdy, Mirv. It's nice to know somebody
else is wasting money.

ANDRÉ FRANCOIS/*France*

ROCKY...

WHAT IS IT NOW, JERRY'?

TELL ME ABOUT THE ECONOMY, ROCKY.

I TOLD YOU YESTER-DAY JERRY.

TELL ME AGAIN, ROCKY. TELL ME AGAIN!

WE ARE A GREAT COUNTRY, JERRY. THE REASON WE ARE GREAT IS BECAUSE WE LIVE IN A FREE ECONOMY. BE-CAUSE IT IS A FREE ECON-OMY IT BELONGS TO THE PEOPLE..

BECAUSE IT BELONGS TO THE PEOPLE, THE PEOPLE CAN BUY IT UP. THE PEO-PLE WHO BOUGHT IT UP ARE LAURANCE, DAVID AND ME.

WHAT ABOUT PRESI-DENT NIXON? DOES HE KNOW THAT, ROCKY?

THERE IS NO PRESIDENT NIXON, JERRY. **YOU** ARE PRESIDENT NOW.

HA HA HA HA HA HA HA HA HA HA THATS FUNNY, ROCKY! HA HA HA HA HA HA HA HA

SHUT UP AND SKI, JERRY.

Field Newspaper Syndicate, 1975

3-16 ©1975 JULES FEIFFER

FEIFFER

JULES FEIFFER/*Field Newspaper Syndicate*

1976

BICENTENNIAL: The entire nation had a euphoric two-hundredth birthday party—the most spectacular event, Op-Sail in New York Harbor, featured an armada of 225 sailing ships from 31 nations. *NATIONAL AFFAIRS:* President Gerald Ford presented congress with the largest defense budget in history in reaction to Russia's growing military capabilities. Dependence on Middle East oil grew and OPEC continued its price increases.

PRIMARIES: Starting out as Jimmy Who?, Carter built an early lead over ten other candidates to hold off strong but late challenges from Jerry Brown and Frank Church for the Democratic nomination. Hubert Humphrey waited in vain for his party's call. At the Republican convention, Ford barely defeated Ronald Reagan, the results hinging on the last 100 uncommitted delegates. *ELECTION:* The campaign featured three televised Ford-Carter debates. In the closest electoral vote in 60 years, Carter wrested the White House from Ford and became the first president from the deep south, despite an indiscreet *Playboy* interview of the Baptist deacon ("I've looked on a lot of women with lust").

SCANDALS: Lockheed Aircraft admitted paying millions of dollars in bribes to win lucrative contracts abroad. In Washington, Elizabeth Ray revealed that she performed more sexual than secretarial duties on the staff of Congressman Wayne Hayes.

AFRICA: Crack Israeli commandos, in a daring air strike, rescued 104 hostages held by Palestinian terrorists at Uganda's Entebbe Airport under the nose of Idi Amin. The black guerrilla war accelerated in Rhodesia. Cuban-Russian intervention increased in Angola and violent rioting erupted in Soweto, the worst in apartheid South Africa's history. Ian Smith resisted demands for black majority rule in Rhodesia.

HUMOR: Secretary Earl Butz resigned after telling a derogatory and tasteless joke about Blacks. *TRAVEL:* Viking I and II landed on Mars, and to the chagrin of science fiction writers, no evidence of life was found. The controversial Concorde SST made its maiden flight despite mass protests by environmentalists. *SPORTS:* Politics intruded into the Montreal Olympics. The Republic of China (Taiwan), denied national participation, went home, as did many African states in protest over South African racial policies.

DEATHS: China lost its revered leaders Mao Tse-tung and Chou En-lai. Mao's widow was arrested for conspiring to seize power with the Gang of Four. Thirty-five people died after swine flu innoculations, bringing the $135 million program to an abrupt halt. Billionaire Howard Hughes died proving he had been alive. A flurry of last Hughes wills surfaced, including one from cartoonist Ed Fischer (see Page 133). Richard Daley and Paul Robeson also died.

INTERLANDI ©1976, LOS ANGELES TIMES

HAPPY BIRTHDAY, AMERICA!

FRANK INTERLANDI/*Los Angeles Times*

THE DEMOCRATS' DONKEY

JEAN-CLAUDE SUARES/New York Times

FEIFFER

JULES FEIFFER/Field Newspaper Syndicate

JURG SPAHR (JUSP)
Bruckenbauer, Switzerland

HAPPY ANNIVERSARY!

"IT'S INCONCEIVABLE TO ME THAT ANYONE WOULD THINK HE COULD DO THIS JOB, THE PRESIDENCY, IF HE COULDN'T CALL ON GOD FOR HELP AND HAVE FAITH THAT HE'D BE GRANTED THAT HELP."
— TIME 5/17/76

I NEVER ACTUALLY SPOKE TO GOD BUT ONCE, WHEN I HIT MY HEAD GETTING OFF A PLANE, I THINK I SAW HIM. HE WAS VERY NICE.

WHITE HOUSE PRAYER BREAKFASTS ARE NOT ENOUGH...WE MUST BRING GOD HIMSELF INTO GOVERNMENT, PREFERABLY IN A HIGH CABINET POST.

THANKS TO MY DOCTRINE OF "LOWER EXPECTATIONS" MY FIRST MEETING WITH GOD WAS NOT A DISAPPOINTMENT.

NU? GO FIGURE IT !? THE DEVIL GETS H.L. MENCKEN, GEORGE BERNARD SHAW, SAM CLEMENS, BILLIE HOLIDAY, GERSHWIN, PORTER, SCHUBERT...AND... AND I....I KEEP GETTING DRECK LIKE THIS !!!

ED SOREL/*New York Village Voice*

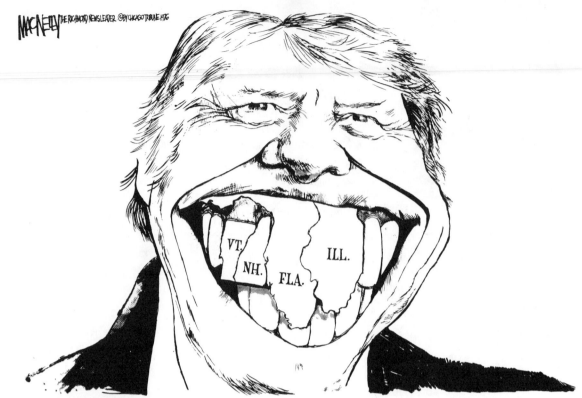

JEFF MacNELLY/*Richmond News-Leader*

JOHN BRANCH/*Chapel Hill Newspaper*

*No more primaries.
I can't take another primary.*

BEN WICKS/*Toronto Telegram, Canada*

BRUCE STARK/New York News

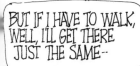

DON WRIGHT/Miami News

SANDY HUFFAKER/*New York Times*

BYRON HUMPHREY/*New Orleans States-Item*

KEN ALEXANDER/ *San Francisco Examiner*

SAM RAWLS (SCRAWLS)/*Atlanta Journal*

ALL THINGS TO ALL PEOPLE

CHARLES BROOKS, *Birmingham News*

DANA FRADON/*The New Yorker*

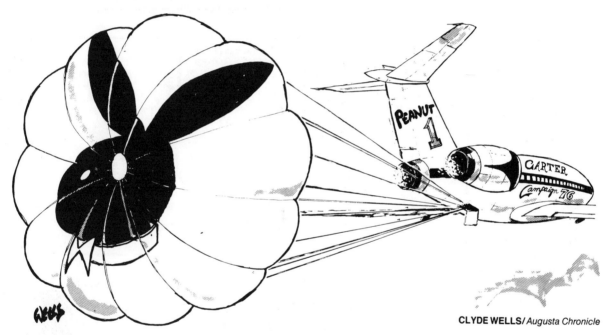

CLYDE WELLS/ *Augusta Chronicle*

THE PRESIDENTIAL CAMPAIGN

JEAN-JACQUES SEMPÉ/ *Paris*

ROBERT ENGLEHART/*Dayton Journal Herald*

DOONESBURY

DIRECT FROM PHILADELPHIA— THE PRESIDENTIAL DEBATES!

TONIGHT'S DEBATE IS BEING BROADCAST LIVE FROM THE WALNUT STREET THEATRE, WHICH HAS BEEN CHILLED TO A PREVIOUSLY AGREED UPON TEMPERATURE OF 68°F!

IN THE INTERESTS OF FAIRNESS, BOTH CANDIDATES HAVE BEEN MADE UP AND LIT IN EXACTLY THE SAME WAY. THEY'RE ALSO SITTING BEHIND MATCHING LECTERNS, AND ARE WEARING IDENTICAL BLUE SUITS!

NOW, THEN, WHICH OF YOU IS GOVERNOR CARTER? HA,HA! HA,HA! I AM.

GARY TRUDEAU/*Universal Press Syndicate*

YOU KNOW WHERE I STAND...

MIKE PETERS/*Dayton Daily News*

DICK WRIGHT/ *Providence Journal-Bulletin*

CLYDE WELLS/ *Augusta Chronicle*

STILL LIFE

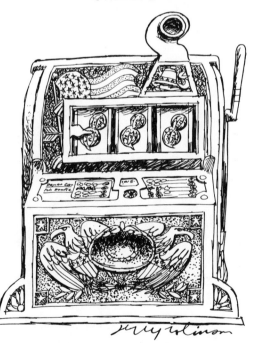

JERRY ROBINSON/ *Cartoonists & Writers Syndicate*

ROBERT GRAYSMITH/ *San Francisco Chronicle*

MIKE PETERS/ *Dayton Daily News*

CARLOS AUGUSTO SOARES (CULICUT)/*O Globo, Brazil*

KENNETH MAHOOD/*Punch, London*

THE WAR AND INFLATION

TOMI UNGERER/*New York Times*

THE ARMS RACE

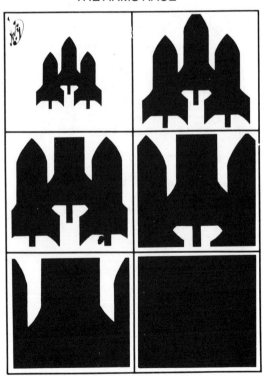

TOM DARCY/*Long Island Newsday*

KEN ALEXANDER/*San Francisco Examiner*

SECY. EARL BUTZ TELLS
AN ETHNIC JOKE

© 1976 NYT SPECIAL FEATURES

DON WRIGHT/*Miami News*

DWANE POWELL/*Raleigh News & Observer*

THE *REAL* HUGHES WILL

Omaha World-Herald
The Newspaper of the Midlands

May 12, 1976

To whom it may concern:
I leave all my money to
editorial cartoonist Ed Fischer
whose cartoons gave me a lift
while I stayed in my
secret hideaway at the
Hilton Hotel in Omaha.
Signed,
Howard Huges

ED FISCHER/*Omaha World Herald*

LOCKHEED

POUL HOLCK/*Däg Bladet Politiken, Denmark*

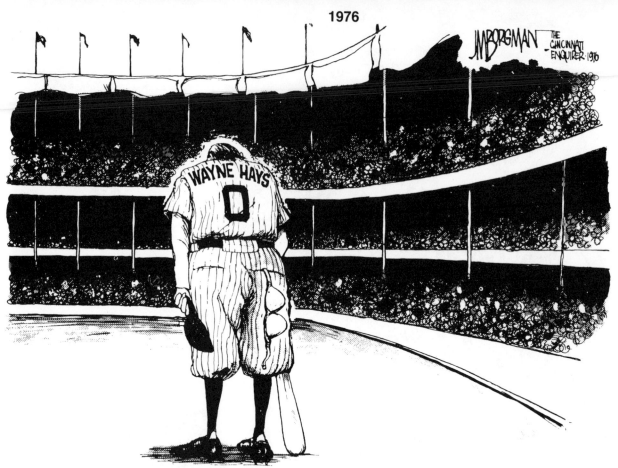

JIM BORGMAN/*Cincinnati Enquirer*

JOHN FISCHETTI/*Chicago Daily News*

TOM DARCY/*Long Island Newsday*

ROBERT ENGLEHART/*Dayton Journal Herald*

TERRY MOSHER (AISLIN)
Montreal Gazette

JUBILEE

CANADA'S SONNY AND CHER

HECTOR VALDES/*El Heraldo de Mexico, Mexico City*

BLAINE/*Hamilton Spectator, Canada*

H. JO EGGSTEIN/*V.B.K., East Germany*

NICOLAS PECAREFF/*Starchel, Bulgaria*

GENERAL PINOCHET

To hold this position we'll need more ammo, more rations . . . and a calculator.

ETTA HULME/*Fort Worth Star-Telegram*

MOHAMMED REZA PAHLEVI

EWERT KARLSSON (EWK)/*Aftonbladet, Sweden*

TONY AUTH/*Philadelphia Inquirer*

BERT WHITMAN/*Phoenix Gazette*

ROMA

N. H. VISSCHER/*Nieuwsblad V.H. Norrden, Holland*

JOHN LANE/*Newspaper Enterprises Association*

Fool! You'll destroy everything we've built together.

MAO & CHOU

FRANCISCO GRAELLS (PANCHO) *El Nacional, Venezuela*

EWERT KARLSSON (EWK)/*Aftonbladet, Sweden*

IAN SMITH

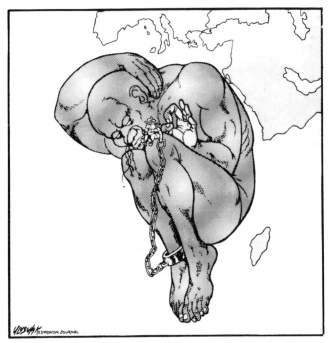

EDD ULUSCHAK/*Edmonton Journal, Canada*

EDMONDO BIGANTI/*O Estado De São Paulo, Brazil*

HANS-GEORG RAUCH/*West Germany*

LOU MYERS/*Politicks Magazine*

CLAUDE FAVARD (BONNET)/*Opus International, France*

RADIVOJ GVOZDANOVIC/*Yugoslavia*

ZORAN JOVANOVIC/*Illujstovana Politika, Yugoslavia*

ISMET VOLJEVICA/*Vecernji List, Yugoslavia*

JEAN-CLAUDE SUARES/*New York Times*

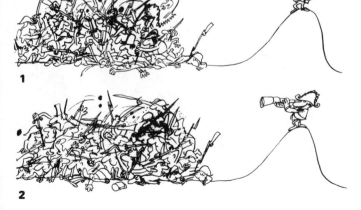

FERENC SAJDIK/*Ludas Matyi, Hungary*

We know you're in there . . . throw out your gun
and come out with your hands up.

RAYMOND LOWRY/*Punch, England*

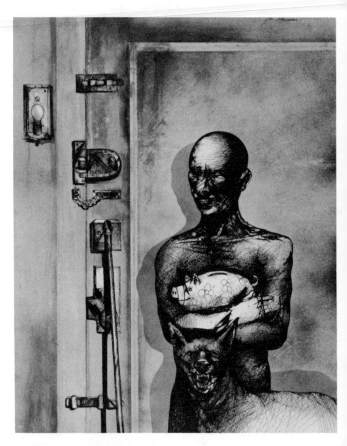

MARSHALL ARISMAN/*Frozen Images*

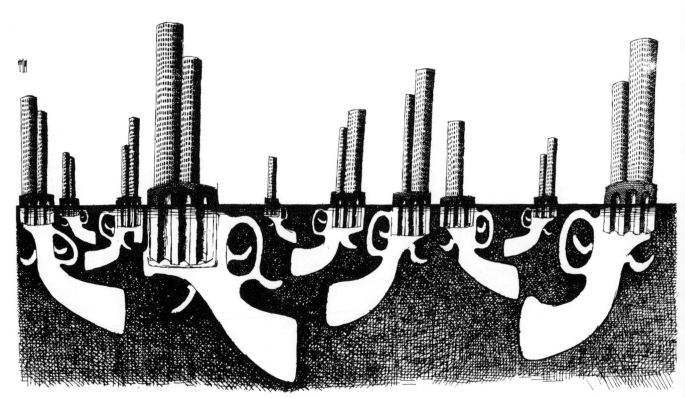

LOUIS MITLBERG (TIM)/*Paris-Match, France*

Sometimes, Carstairs, I wonder if it's worth it.

MARTIN HONEYSETT/*Punch, London*

JOSE LUIS MARTIN MENA/*El Ideal Gallego, Spain*

JOHNNY BEKAERT (STROP)/*Knack, Belgium*

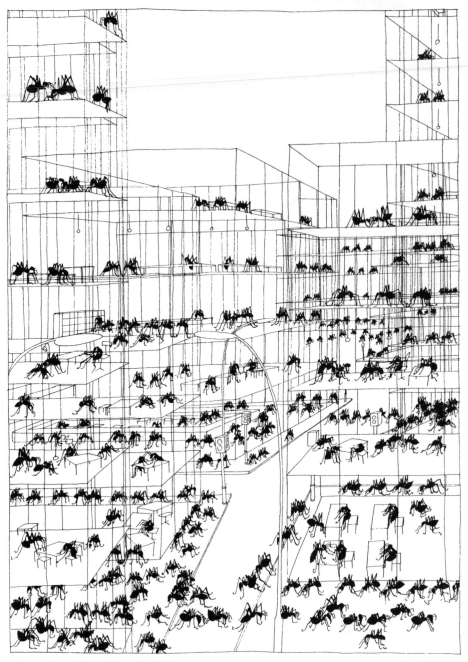

HANS-GEORG RAUCH/ *West Germany*

ON THIS SITE WILL BE
ERECTED A 32-STORY
LUXURY BUILDING
AFTER THE DEMISE OF
THE OLD LADY

CHARLES ADDAMS/ *New Yorker Magazine*

AHMET SABUNCU/ *Turkey*

BALAZS BALAZS-PIRI/ *Ludas Matyi, Hungary*

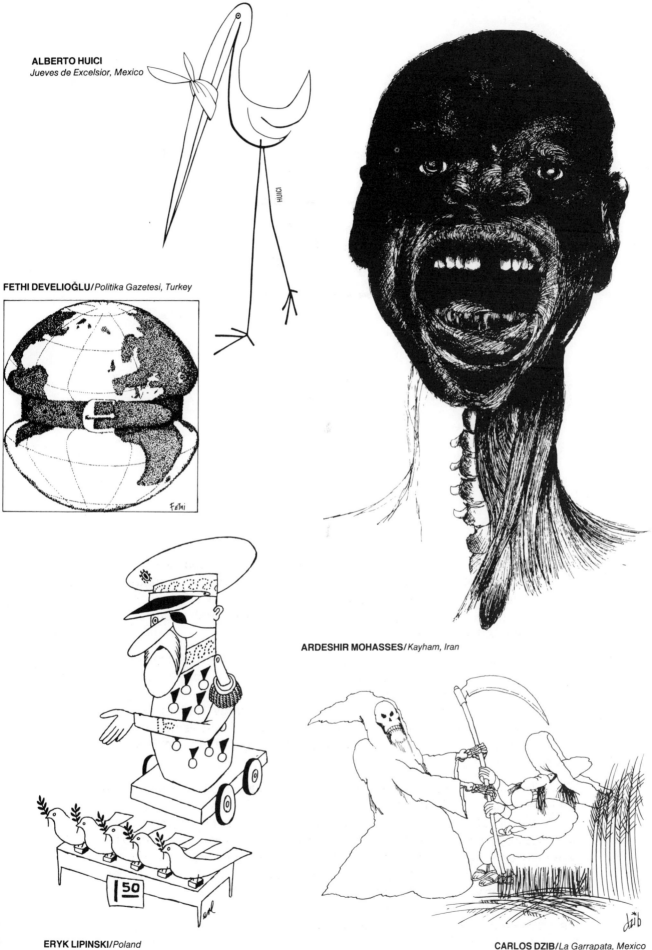

ALBERTO HUICI
Jueves de Excelsior, Mexico

FETHI DEVELIOĞLU/ *Politika Gazetesi, Turkey*

ARDESHIR MOHASSES/ *Kayham, Iran*

ERYK LIPINSKI/ *Poland*

CARLOS DZIB/ *La Garrapata, Mexico*

1977

NEAR EAST: Egyptian President Anwar Sadat made an historic pilgrimage to Israel, the first visit by an Arab leader to the Jewish state. A dialogue began with Prime Minister Menachem Begin over Palestinian self-determination and return of captured Arab land. PLO leader Arafat and other Arab heads of state denounced Sadat's initiative.

CARTER: The new President's honeymoon was short-lived. A Democratic Congress resisted many of his proposals, among them: a $50 tax rebate, a gasoline tax, voter registration, a new consumer agency, and government reorganization—but he did get a new Department of Energy. Carter postponed production of the B-1 bomber and voiced hope for a SALT II agreement in 1978. Andrew Young became the most controversial member of the administration after a series of intemperate remarks.

SCANDALS: Bert Lance, a Carter crony and his budget director, resigned after an investigation revealed questionable banking practices by him as a Georgia bank executive. Tongsun Park, a generous South Korean rice merchant, was indicted for bribing dozens of Congressmen, thereby adding a new word to the Washington lexicon—Koreagate. CRIME: John Mitchell, Nixon's Attorney General, received a 2½ to 8 year sentence for his role in the Watergate scandals. Garry Gilmore's death wish was fulfilled in the first U.S. execution since 1967. World-wide terrorism became a growing concern to many nations as it threatened their internal stability and international relations.

TONY AUTH/*Philadelphia Inquirer*

TREATY: Carter and General Omar Torrijos signed the Panama Canal Treaty but strong opposition made its ratification by the Senate debatable. *GAY RIGHTS:* Anita Bryant, an orange juice spokesperson, led a successful campaign to repeal a Miami ordinance that prohibited discrimination against homosexuals. *AFRICA:* Russia took advantage of a continent in racial and policital turmoil to extend its influence. Convulsions shook Ethiopia, Somalia, Angola, and Rhodesia. In Uganda, President Idi Amin Dada's repulsive regime survived a coup attempt, and news of the death of black leader Steve Biko as a result of police beatings set off bloody riots in South Africa.

ENERGY: The 800-mile, $7.7-billion trans-Alaskan pipeline opened, but did little to quench America's insatiable thirst for gasoline. *HEALTH:* While Congress debated using federal funds for abortion, millions of dollars in Medicare and Medicaid frauds were uncovered. Doctor and hospital costs skyrocketed.

BILLY CARTER: The President's brother exploited his relationship, earning over $500,000 in various enterprises, including Billy Beer, his favorite beverage. *TELEVISION:* Richard Nixon received $600,000 plus a percentage of the profits for a series of interviews with David Frost, and *Roots,* an epic of Black history by Alex Haley, attracted one of the largest audiences in history.

DEATHS: Anthony Eden, Dr. Wernher von Braun, Bing Crosby, Charles Chaplin, Elvis Presley, Groucho Marx, Zero Mostel, Rosalind Russell, Joan Crawford, Leopold Stokowski, Guy Lombardo, and Li'l Abner, age 43.

BILL GARNER/_Memphis Commercial Appeal_

OH SURE, YOU WERE IN ISRAEL OVER THE WEEKEND.... PROBABLY REVIEWING THEIR TROOPS, RIGHT?.... HAVING DINNER WITH BEGIN AND GOLDA, RIGHT?....

MIKE PETERS/_Dayton Daily News_

PETE HIRONAKA/_Pacific Citizen_

ANTON DRAGOS/_Flacara, Roumania_

DAVID SUTER/_New York Times_

1977

BYRON HUMPHREY
New Orleans States-Item

ARNOLD ROTH/*Punch, London*

RONALD REAGAN HEARS A PANAMANIAN SPIT IN OUR CANAL

One!

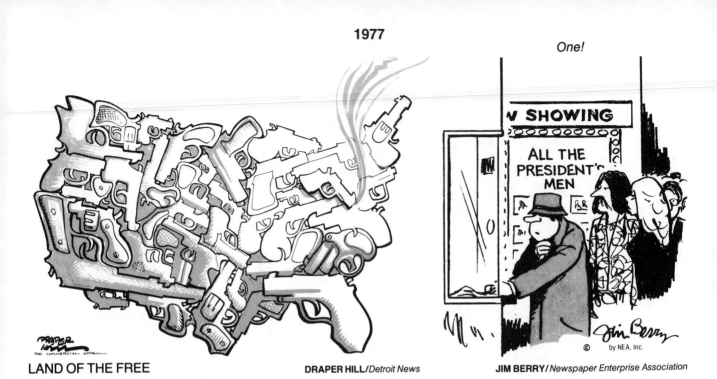

LAND OF THE FREE

DRAPER HILL/*Detroit News*

JIM BERRY/ *Newspaper Enterprise Association*

JOHN MITCHELL, BEFORE AND AFTER

ED SOREL/*New York Village Voice*

You've got Richard Nixon to kick around again!

HY ROSEN/Albany Times Union

JOHN TREVER/Albuquerque Journal

DAVID FROST AND RICHARD NIXON

DAVID LEVINE/New York Review of Books

LIFE WITH ROBINSON

JERRY ROBINSON/*Cartoonists & Writers Syndicate*

JEFF MacNELLY/*Richmond News-Leader*

MIKE PETERS/*Dayton Daily News*

ED FISCHER/*Omaha World Herald*

This is the President! Throw out your rubber stamps . . .
I have you surrounded!

ROBERT GRAYSMITH/ *San Francisco Chronicle*

JAMES MORIN/ *Miami Herald*

BEN SARGENT/ *Austin American Star*

THE REPUBLICAN NATIONAL COMMITTEE MEETS
TO CONSIDER A NEW PARTY SYMBOL

ARNOLD ROTH/*Politicks Magazine*

NEWS ITEM: POPE PAUL AGAINST WOMEN BECOMING PRIESTS

TERRY MOSHER (AISLIN)/*Montreal Gazette*

Inquisition.

THE **NORMAL** HAVE NOTHING TO FEAR.

THE **NORMAL** HAVE NOTHING TO FEAR.

THE **NORMAL** HAVE NOTHING TO FEAR.

THE **NORMAL** HAVE NOTHING TO FEAR.

BEN SARGENT/*Austin American Star*

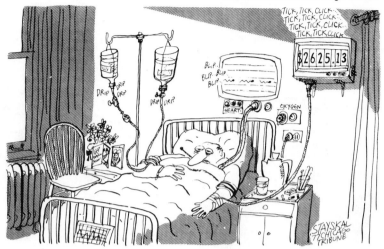

WAYNE STAYSKAL/*Chicago Tribune*

PAUL CONRAD/*Los Angeles Times*

NEWS ITEM: ONE OUT OF EVERY THREE DOCTORS PAID UNDER MEDICAL PLANS FOUND CHEATING ON INCOME TAX

JAWS!

ROGELIO NARANJO/*Actualidad, Mexico*

CHARLES WERNER/*Indianapolis Star*

PAUL SZEP/*Boston Globe*

MICHAEL KEEFE/*Denver Post*

ANOTOLI ONANOV OF RUSSIA IS 106 YEARS OLD.

TO WHAT DOES HE CREDIT HIS LONG LIFE?

I HAFF NEVER CRITICIZED THE STATE.

ROBERT ENGLEHART/*Dayton Journal Herald*

CHUCK AYERS/*Akron Beacon Journal*

CLYDE WELLS/ *Augusta Chronicle*

Oops!

I am not a crook . . . I'm a banker.

PAUL SZEP/ *Boston Globe*

STAINED GLASS

KARL HUBENTHAL/ *Los Angeles Herald-Examiner*

1977

ELVIS

JAMES MORIN/*Miami Herald*

LOU GRANT/*Oakland Tribune*

BING

JAN O. HENRIKSEN (JANO)/*Faedrelandsvennen, Norway*

THE END

ROB LAWLOR/*Philadelphia Daily News*

ZERO MOSTEL

I would never join a club that would accept me as a member.

PAUL CONRAD/*Los Angeles Times*

1978

CAMP DAVID: Jimmy Carter took Menachem Begin and Anwar Sadat to the presidential retreat and after thirteen days of intensive negotiations came down from the summit with the Camp David Accords, generally acclaimed, except by the Communist and Arab rejectionist states, as an historic step toward Mid-East peace.

DECISIONS: The Senate, after bitter debate, ratified the Panama Canal Treaties by a narrow margin. Carter postponed production of the neutron bomb and announced recognition of the People's Republic of China, cutting Taiwan adrift. The Supreme Court, in a 5 to 4 decision in the landmark Allan Bakke case, upheld affirmative-action admission plans in universities but struck down rigidly drawn guotas. Other decisions by the Burger court were seen as limiting freedom of the press under the first amendment. TAXES: California voters passed the controversial Proposition 13, brainchild of Howard Jarvis, cutting $7 billion in property taxes. Fiscal conservatism became de rigueur for politicians nationwide.

VATICAN: Pope Paul VI died at 80. After only 34 days as Pontiff, his successor, Pope John Paul I, too, was dead. The College of Cardinals then elected the first non-Italian Pope in 455 years: Polish Cardinal Karol Wojtyla, Pope John Paul II. IRAN: Bloody riots by anti-Shah Muslim Fundamentalists, led by the exiled Ayatollah Khomeini in Paris, paralyzed the country and crippled oil production. AFRICA: Ethiopia, employing Cuban forces, fought invading Somalis in the

FEIFFER

JULES FEIFFER/*Field Newspaper Syndicate*

disputed Ogaden region. *RUSSIA:* Dissidents Shcharansky, Ginzburg, and Orlow were sentenced to long prison terms.

HEALTH: Chemical drums buried thirty years ago in the Love Canal near Niagara Falls became a toxic time bomb fueling a growing national controversy over industrial and nuclear waste disposal. *TRAGEDIES:* Former Italian Premier Aldo Moro was kidnapped and murdered by Red Brigade terrorists. In Guyana, Jim Jones, the charismatic leader of the Poeple's Temple, first caused the assassination of a U.S. Congressman, then lead 918 followers in a grisly mass murder/suicide. Masses of Indochinese refugee "boat people" in make-shift craft fled Communist regimes. Thousands died at sea as many nations refused them safe harbor and set them adrift.

FIRSTS: Louise Brown, the "test-tube baby," was born in England, the first child conceived outside her mother's body. Muhammad Ali defeated Leon Spinks and became the first to win the heavyweight boxing championship three times. The first Atlantic balloon crossing was made by three Americans. Scientists were skeptical of the claim in a book, *In His Image,* that the first cloning, reproduction using the cell from only one parent, had already taken place. King Tut made his first and only transatlantic crossing in 4,000 years to visit the U.S.

DEATHS: Hubert Horatio Humphrey, Margaret Mead, Jomo Kenyatta, Golda Meir, Norman Rockwell, Edgar Bergen.

ROBERT PRYOR/*Los Angeles Times*

TONY AUTH/*Philadelphia Inquirer*

BEGIN PROPOSES A PEACE PLAN

G. EHRLICH (GUS)/*TV Antenne 2, France*

LIFE WITH ROBINSON

JERRY ROBINSON/*Cartoonists & Writers Syndicate*

MARC PODUAL/ *New York Times*

CONFLICT: ALGERIA-MOROCCO

G. EHRLICH (GUS)/ *TV Antenne 2, France*

JOSÉ HERNANDEZ/ *Tiempo de Cordoba, Argentina*

FROST OVER KREMLIN

THE TERRORISTS ALWAYS AIM
FOR THE LEGS

EWERT KARLSSON (EWK)/Aftonbladet, Sweden

SCOTT LONG/Minneapolis Tribune

NICOLAI KAPUSTA/ Radjanska Donetchyna, USSR

1978

LATEST OFFERING

GENE BASSET/ *Scripps-Howard Newspapers*

Opposition to the right of me!
Opposition to. the left of me!
Opposition in front of me!
Jimmy Carter behind me . . .
I think. . . .

HUGH HAYNIE/ *Louisville Courier-Journal*

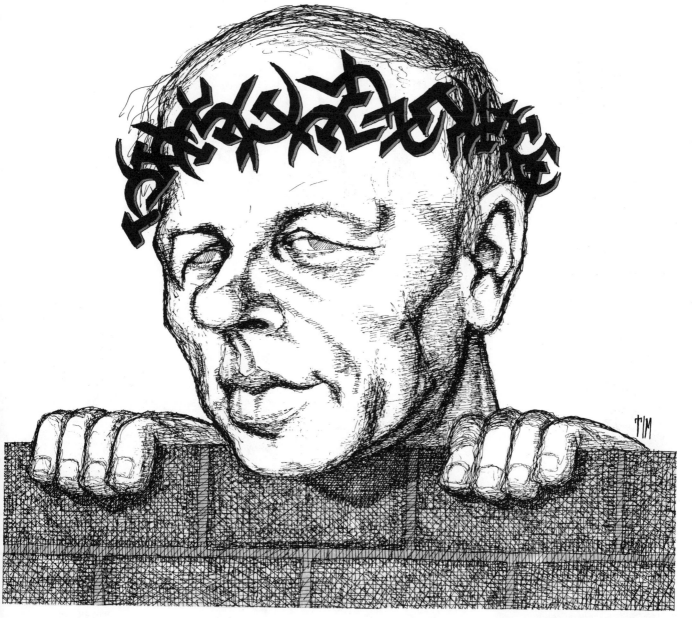

LOUIS MITLBERG (TIM)/ *Paris-Match, France*

JERRY ROBINSON/Cartoonists & Writers Syndicate

TIM MENEES (TIMENEES)/ Pittsburgh Post-Gazette

MARINO/Excelsior, Mexico

HELIOFLORES/ El Universal, Mexico

JAMES MORIN/ Miami Herald

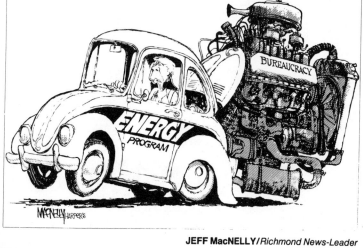

JEFF MacNELLY/*Richmond News-Leader*

THE ENERGY CRISIS IN THE U.S.

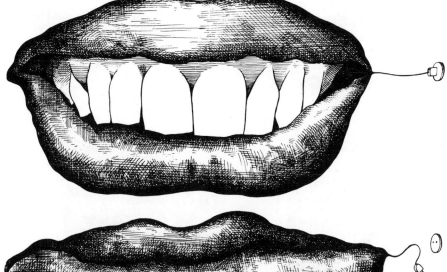

FRANCISCO GRAELLS (PANCHO)
El Nacional, Venezuela

ANTONIO MOREIRA ANTUNES/*Expresso, Portugal*

ROBERT ENGLEHART/*Dayton Journal Herald*

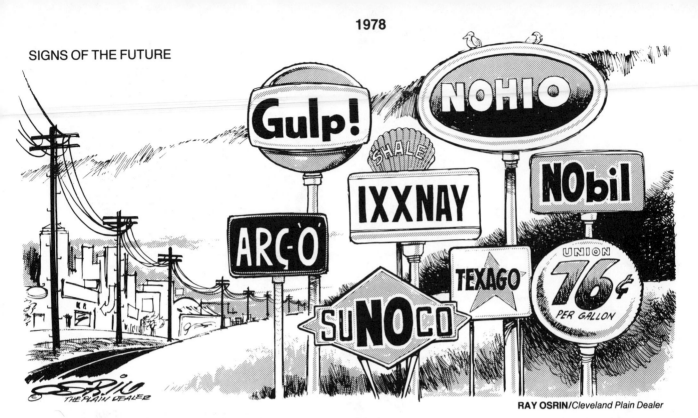

SIGNS OF THE FUTURE

RAY OSRIN/*Cleveland Plain Dealer*

COLLECTORS ITEM

HANK BRENNAN/*Newsweek*

O. PASQUIM/*Brazil*

CRUDE OIL

LOU GRANT/*Oakland Tribune*

ROBERT SULLIVAN/*Worcester Telegram*

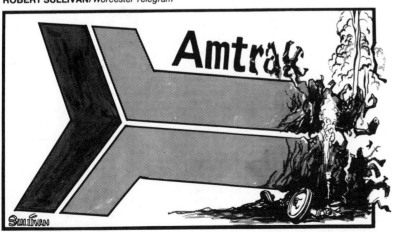

1978

ROBERT PRYOR/*Los Angeles Times*

TIMOTHY ATSEFF/*Syracuse Journal & American*

HANS SIGG/*Tages Anzeiger, Jugoslavia*

THE FALCONER

KARL HUBENTHAL/*Los Angeles Herald-Examiner*

"THE WINNER!"

GENE BASSET/*Scripps-Howard Newspapers*

169

NATIVITY

STEVE GREENBERG/*Van Nuys Valley News*

JACK JURDEN/*Wilmington News Journal*

ART BIMROSE/*Portland Oregonian*

LIFE WITH ROBINSON

JERRY ROBINSON/*Cartoonists & Writers Syndicate*

PAUL CONRAD/ *Los Angeles Times*

CHUCK AYERS/ *Akron Beacon Journal*

JERRY FEARING/ *St. Paul Dispatch*

JAMES MORIN/ *Miami Herald*

1979

NUCLEAR ENERGY: A potentially catastrophic accident at Three-Mile Island nuclear power plant near Middletown, Pennsylvania, threatened a core melt-down ("China Syndrome") and massive loss of life.

Iran: Shah Reza Pahlavi was forced to leave his country after thirty-seven years on the Peacock throne. Exiled Ayatollah Khomeini returned to Iran to establish an Islamic Republic. The revolutionary council executed hundreds of former officials. Admitting the Shah to the U.S. for medical treatment triggered violent anti-American demonstrations in Teheran. On November 4, a student mob seized the U.S. embassy, taking over 50 Americans hostage. Several Blacks and women were released but demands made for the others included the return of the Shah and his fortune.

OVERTHROWN: Cambodia's Pol Pot, Uganda's Idi Amin, Nicaragua's President Somoza. *CANADA:* Joe Clark ended Pierre Trudeau's rule as Prime Minister and Quebec Premier Rene Levesque sought a mandate for secession. *BRITAIN:* Margaret Thatcher became the first woman Prime Minister and Earl Mountbatten was assassinated in renewed I.R.A. terrorism.

WAR & PEACE: Over 200,000 Chinese troops invaded Vietnam but withdrew after less than one month with heavy losses. Egyptian President Sadat and Israeli Prime Minister Begin signed a formal peace treaty, ending the 31 years state of war. *TRAVEL:* Deputy Premier Deng Xiaoping visited the U.S. as trade relations were expanded with American companies, led by Coca Cola. Pope John Paul II journeyed to Mexico, his native Poland, Ireland and the U.S.

CARTER: The President held a ten-day Domestic Summit at Camp David. U.N. Ambassador Andrew Young and five members of the cabinet resigned. Carter's popularity polls dropped to a record low until the Iran crisis resulted in a dramatic rise. Ten Republicans, including Ronald Reagan, announced their presidential candidacy. Senator Ted Kennedy posed a threat to Carter's re-nomination but his campaign was plagued by the media's focus on Chappaquiddick.

DETENTE: Salt II was signed by Carter and Brezhnev but Russia's invasion of Afghanistan put the treaty in jeopardy. *SKYLAB:* The 77-ton space station spread debris over Australia in its plunge to earth. *KKK:* Increased Ku Klux Klan activity induced violence in Alabama.

ECONOMY: The recession and continuing energy crisis triggered an historic rise in gold prices, erosion of the dollar, record interest rates, 13.5% inflation, 5.8% unemployment, and a Wall Street selling panic. Chrysler faced bankruptcy and Amtrak was forced to sharply reduce service. Exxon and other oil companies, however, reported billions in profits, some exceeding a 200% increase.

DEATHS: Nelson Rockefeller, Arthur Fiedler, Emmett Kelly, Gene Tunney, A. Philip Randolph, John Wayne, S. J. Perelman, Al Capp.

PAUL CONRAD/*Los Angeles Times*

WALTER HANEL/*Deutsche Zeitung, Germany*

MIHAI STÁNESCU/*Roumania*

GABOR BENEDEK (BEN) *Suddeutsche Zeitung, Meinungen, Germand*

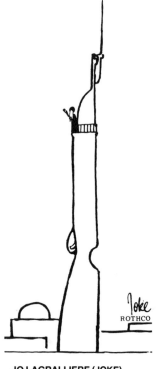

JO LAGRALLIERE (JOKE)
De Nieuwe-Gazet, Belgium

JARL-ERIC BERGLUNG (JEB)
Goteborgs-Tidningen, Sweden

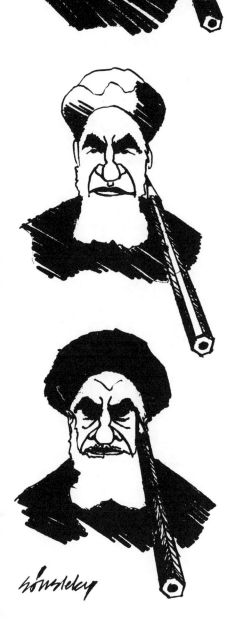

VEN SONSLEBY/*Nä Magazine, Norway*

PAT OLIPHANT
Washington Star

Of course, I'd resign at once if I thought for a moment they really meant it!

JAMES MORIN/ *Miami Herald*

1979

GUSTAV PEICHL (IRONIMUS)/*Die Presse, Austria*

MAHAMMUD KAHIL/*Arab News, Saudi Arabia*

EDGAR SOLLER/*Philippines Daily Express, Philippines*

FRITS MULLER/*Haagse Post, Holland*

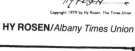

17th century

Copyright 1979 by Hy Rosen, The Times-Union

HY ROSEN/*Albany Times Union*

ARDESHIR MOHASSES/ *Kayham, Iran*

BAS MITROPOULOS (BAS)/*Greece*

HOSTAGES!

CHARLES WERNER/*Indianapolis Star*

LOUIS MITLBERG (TIM)/*Paris-Match, France*

ROBERT PRYOR/_Los Angeles Times_

DON WRIGHT/_Miami News_

MR. PRESIDENT, YOU COMPARED YOURSELF WITH SENATOR KENNEDY BY SAYING YOU WOULD NOT PANIC IN A CRISIS. IS THIS A REFERENCE TO CHAPPAQUIDDICK?

ABSOLUTELY NOT! I COULDN'T RUN THAT KIND OF CAMPAIGN. CHAPPAQUIDDICK IS NOT AN ISSUE HERE!

THAT'S C-H-A-P-P-A-Q-

I'm worried—this group could make that joker inside look half-way good!

PAT OLIPHANT/_Washington Star_

BILL SCHORR/ *Kansas City Star*

JAMES MORIN/ *Miami Herald*

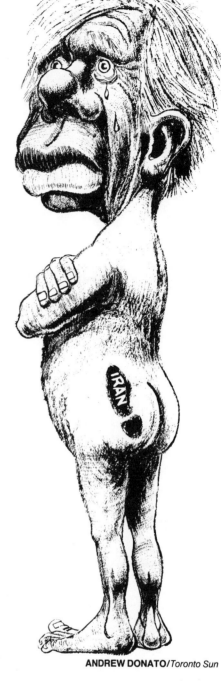

ANDREW DONATO/ *Toronto Sun*

DOONESBURY

GARY TRUDEAU/ *Universal Press Syndicate*

PAUL RIGBY/ *New York Past*

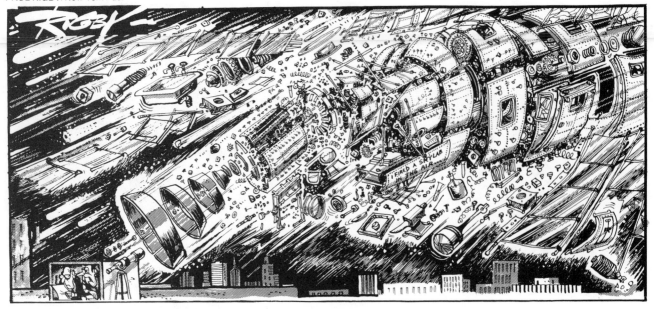

And what are the odds against being hit by TWO pieces!

IT WON'T GO AWAY

JIM BORGMAN/*Cincinnati Enquirer*

EVOLUTION

SUMMERS

1979 THE FAYETTEVILLE TIMES

DANA SUMMERS/*Fayetteville Times*

UNCLE SAM'S MERCY MISSION
SOUP FOR THE DESTITUTE

CHRYSLER

PAT CROWLEY/*Palm Beach Post*

POPE VISITS U.S.

Schlitz Beer

AISLIN 79
MONTREAL GAZETTE

TERRY MOSHER (AISLIN)/*Montreal Gazette*

BOB TAYLOR/ *Dallas Times Herald*

RICHARD ALLISON/ *St. Joseph Gazette*

JAWS 2

ONE GOOD BITE DESERVES ANOTHER!

ROBERT SINET (SINÉ)/ *Paris*

JANUSZ MAJEWSKI (MAYK)
Sydsvenska Dagbladet, Sweden

PURCHASING POWER OF DOLLAR CONTINUES DECLINE
BYRON HUMPHREY/ *New Orleans States-Item*

LOU MYERS/_Politicks Magazine_

ALL RIGHT, GIRLS... ONCE MORE, WITH FEELING ... **HELL NO, WE WON'T GO!**

KATE PALMER/_Greenville News_

WAYNE STAYSKAL/_Chicago Tribune_

ROBERT ENGLEHART/_Dayton Journal Herald_

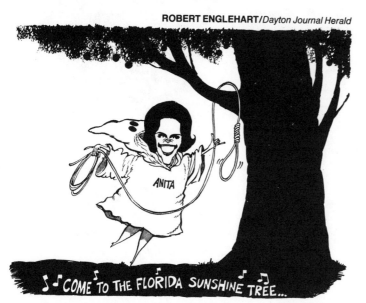

♪ COME TO THE FLORIDA SUNSHINE TREE... ♪

_So what if I have
an abortion, Adam,
who'll ever know?_

THOMAS INNES/Calgary Herald, Canada

ANDREZEJ CZYCZYLO/Szpilki, Poland

NICOLAI KAPUSTA/Radjanska Donetchyna, USSR

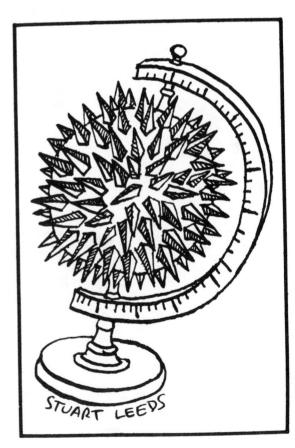

STUART LEEDS/New York Times

ANONYMOUS/ *Krokodil Magazine, U.S.S.R.*

GEORGE FISHER/ *Arkansas Gazette*

CHUCK AYERS/ *Akron Beacon Journal*

ETTA HULME **FORT WORTH STAR-TELEGRAM** N.E.A, '79

ETTA HULME/*Fort Worth Star-Telegram*

NICOLAI KAPUSTA/*Radjanska Donetchyna, USSR*

RICHARD LOCHER/*Chicago Tribune*

PAT CROWLEY/*Palm Beach Post*

ED ASHLEY/*Toledo Blade*

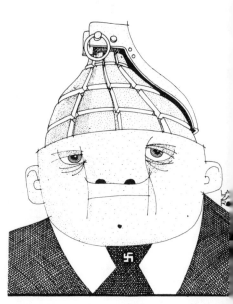

LAZARO FERNANDEZ/*Dedete, Cuba*

MICHAEL KONOPACKI/ *Madison Press Connection*

BAS MITROPOULOS (BAS)/ *Greece*

SANDY CAMPBELL/ *Nashville Tennessean*

We're passing around a petition to keep those Vietnam foreigners out of our community.

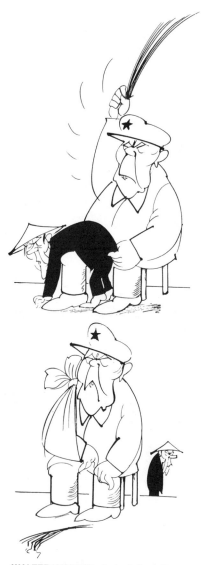

WALTER HANEL/ *Deutsche Zeitung, Germany*

ROGELIO NARANJO/ *Actualidad, Mexico*

M. G. LORD/*Long Island Newsday*

Someday, son, all this will be yours.

EDDIE GERMANO/*Brockton Enterprise*

EDWARD GAMBLE/*Nashville Banner*

Where is everybody?

EWERT KARLSSON (EWK)/*Aftonbladet, Sweden*

DUNCAN MacPHERSON/*Toronto Star*

OSWALDO SAGASTEGUI/*Excelsior, Mexico*

JANUSZ MAJEWSKI (MAYK)/
Sydsvenska Dagbladet, Sweden

BILL DEORE/Dallas News

ROB LAWLOR/Philadelphia Daily News

FAN JIANG/People's Republic of China

NEW MODEL

MARK TAYLOR/Albuquerque Tribune

TONY AUTH/*Philadelphia Inquirer*

ALBERT EINSTEIN, 1879-1955

LOU GRANT/*Oakland Tribune*

TRUE GRIT

PAUL CONRAD/*Los Angeles Times*

Index